REGAINING BALANCE:
The Evolution of the UUA

BY
MICHAEL WERNER

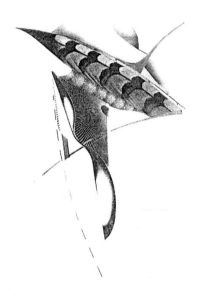

Religious Humanism Press

ISBN: 978-0-9893672-0-2

Published by Religious Humanism Press an imprint of
HUUmanists formerly the Fellowship of Religious Humanism
HUUmanists
P.O. Box 185202
Hamden, CT 06518-0202
http://huumanists.org/
Title page art by Eric Anderson
Printed in the United States of America

Contents

Statement of Purpose
A Distinctive Series of Monographs

This monograph is the first in a series entitled *Voices of Diversity* to be published by Religious Humanism Press. The Unitarian Universalist Fourth Principle calls for a *free and responsible* search for truth and meaning. In the deep conviction that robust dialogue is a sine qua non of an enduring community, this series will provide a forum for Unitarian Universalist authors to express their thoughts, feelings, and positions on important and often controversial topics related to the opportunities and challenges facing the Humanist movement within Unitarian Universalism. The authors will be given editorial latitude to "tell it as they see it." Their opinions and conclusions may or may not reflect the views of members of either the HUUmanists Association or the Editorial Review Board of Religious Humanism Press. This series is intended to provoke dialogue. Accordingly, the Review Board encourages responses from readers and will give such responses wide circulation.

Introduction

THIS PAPER IS about hope and restoration. It is about the need for positive transformation of the Unitarian Universalist Association. It will not always seem so, but underlying this history and critique is the knowledge that there is a better direction for the UUA, a direction of both greater authenticity and growth, a way of tapping into the secular revolution occurring in the United States. I have seen what a fully balanced Humanist community of heart and mind, reason and compassion can look like in the Unitarian Universalist Association (UUA). I have seen transformative, intentionally Humanist communities of balanced full secular lives that embrace our deepest longings in an integrated world view that compromises neither our intellectual integrity nor our emotional power. This paper is a call for the evolution of the UUA with the new realities of the twenty first century. It is a call to offer those coming in on the tidal wave of secularism a future meaningful home that challenges them to greater and deeper lives in the community of others. The UUA can be a powerful guiding force in the future, but only with some radical self-analysis and restoration of our basic mission and focus from some serious missteps.

This paper started just as a history of Humanism in the Unitarian Universalist Association (UUA), but then I realized that a dry academic paper was not going to have any meaningful impact. What I really wanted was an awakening. I wanted change. I and many others have been worried for a long time about the state and future viability of the UUA, Humanism within the UUA, the loss of an important dimension to secular life, and how a narrow ideology has taken over the UUA. I have grieved over these losses and, like many, lost confidence that these issues could be rectified. On reflection I now think they can. A few decades ago I think that the UUA lost its way and entered a retrograde period of unbalanced liberal values where some of our most important values have been not only neglected, but trampled upon. The value of reason in religion has been discarded along with critical thinking, science, and progressive thought. Appreciation for truth has become an imperiled value. We will explore how an ideology of radical tolerance and indiscriminate pluralism skewed the whole conversation, not only in the UUA, but in liberal religion in general. Indeed, we will engage in Unitarian Universalist heresy.

This paper is a tough polemic and as such I fully expect a response that I am arguing for intolerance; not at all. It is not an either/or. What I hope for is a balanced sense of values, a realization that there is no "right" way to do Unitarian Universalism, but there are consequences and skewing our values in any direction necessarily entails losses. When we place one value over all others, it is becomes ideology. The real question is if we have the courage and insight to balance multiple values. It is not a question of tolerance vs. intolerance. Keep tolerance, but restore other values to provide a pathway to balanced progressive growth. It is my yearning for change that will build UUA communities that can challenge and evoke the best in us.

I'll be blunt. Unitarian Universalism is dying. Like someone buried alive we close our eyes and dream of past and future glories and smile. Death is not imminent so we can afford to dream for a while. But not long. We will examine how we reached this point and if there are any possible remedies. Remedies may be too late to save an unwilling patient. If nothing else let this serve as a historical record for any autopsy, not just of the author's viewpoint, but thousands of other concerned UU's. Humanists have been accused of bloodless Rationalism. This analysis will not be so, but it will be a frank discussion of which there have been too few lately.

This paper will describe and critique how the Unitarian Universalist Association (UUA) has evolved in the twentieth century. It will try to put into some perspective the sociological, philosophical, cultural, and marketing momentum that has led to rather dramatic changes in the orientations and the future viability of this important liberal community. My biases, concerns, and feelings of personal loss as a Unitarian Universalist Humanist will be obvious. Still, it does not diminish my overall love, respect and appreciation for an organization that has given so much to me and as such my criticisms are intended primarily as potentially illuminative of existing realties, possible tradeoffs, and possible turning points for the future.

Unitarian Universalism has been taken over by a narrow ideology of toleration, the historical focus on rational religion has been abandoned, and the lack of purpose and focus is resulting in a sharp decline in membership. This paper will discuss the historic reasons for this and possible paths forward. I am primarily speaking to the many ministers who have seen and been disturbed by these trends and hope to empower them. We can't look for help from the denominational leadership who are good, well-meaning people, but have led the UUA in the wrong direction, and it is doubtful they will reverse an entrenched position. The laity, largely interested in their local communities, are mostly unaware of the complex forces and direction, and they remain on the sidelines.

It is sometimes hard to see this decline as many are in healthy, dynamic, and even growing Unitarian Universalist congregations. It is sometimes hard to see the decline in some congregations that have kept the spirit and practice of reason in religion alive and not succumbed to the ideology of radical tolerance on a local level. Individual congregation dynamics only mask the undeniable overall direction of the UUA, and the facts will speak for themselves.

How We Arrived Here –
A Historical Perspective

U NITARIANISM HAS TRADITIONALLY been publicly defined by the concept and practice of freedom of belief, but actually has always been more characterized by its focus on reason in religion. Classical liberalism is based on a three-legged stool of freedom, reason and tolerance. Rights, equality, and justice are also mentioned as substantial values supporting liberalism in the literature.[1] In spite of the official pronouncements to be egalitarian, Unitarianism traditionally has been a progressive elitist tradition pushing the boundaries of liberal thought. Most people who think that the concept of religious tolerance has been the defining characteristic throughout the UUA history are surprised to learn that Unitarianism expressed itself primarily in Christian terms up until the beginning of the twentieth century. For example, "The (nineteenth century) Unitarian patriarchs Clark and F.H. Hedge of Harvard declared that progress beyond Christianity was only backward and downward; all true religious progress was within Christianity." [2]

While tolerance has always been an important facet within Unitarianism, it has only recently become the primary focus surpassing Christianity and, more importantly, rational religion which has been the historic primary characteristic of Unitarianism. In William Ellery Channing's famous Baltimore sermon he objected to "the contemptuous manner in which reason is often spoken of by our adversaries, and he asserted that "truth is decided at the bar of reason." In moving from a faith-based to a rational foundation for religion within the AUA, this sermon reverberated throughout the religious landscape.

Earl Morse Wilbur said in his classic 1925 *Our Unitarian Heritage*, "Freedom may go wild unless it is guided by some wholesome principle. This principle Unitarians have found in the use of reason in religion. To the Unitarian of today the marks of true religion are spiritual freedom, enlightened reason, broad and tolerant sympathy, upright character and selfless service." [3]

According to the 1963 UUA study *A Free Church in a Changing World*, "Tradition is always being reshaped and modified." [4] If anything has been characteristic of religious liberalism, it is the speed with which its traditions are continually reformulated. Here we must give our attention to a key word in religious liberalism - truth. It is ultimately a new vision of truth that moves human beings to reshape their traditions. The history of Unitarians and Universalists resounds with phrases such as, 'discipleship to advancing truth,' 'the authority of truth known or to be known,' 'the universal truths taught by the great prophets and teachers of humanity in every age and tradition.' " [5] A commitment to excellence has also been a primary focus as exemplified by James Freeman Clark's famous fifth point of Unitarian belief, "the progress of mankind onward and upward forever" which was a point of pride for a long time.

Going back, it was only when the Humanists in the late 19th century came on the scene in the Midwest that pressure grew to broaden the theological perspective beyond Christianity. The Western Conference was a collection of those societies, fellowships and churches bent toward a proto-humanism that sprung up along with the humanistic Free Religious Association. They were willing to leave the American Unitarian Association, if need be, to eliminate the official Christian purpose, to have the individual churches truly independent, and to be able to expressly promote non-theism in their congregations. A schism was narrowly averted in 1887 when William Channing Gannett's compromise statement of, "We hold reason and conscience to be final authorities in matters of religious belief," and seriously engaging the rule of polity promised the Western conference churches congregational autonomy. [6] The Christian creedal purpose was dropped.

Humanism, in the non-supernatural form we know it today, originated and was given powerful voice in Western Conference churches led by leaders such as John Dietrich, Curtis Reese, and Charles Francis Potter when they called for an explicit and forceful evolution of the AUA to a rational, naturalistic metaphysics. They were unequivocal and unapologetic in saying Unitarianism needed to move forward out of the theistic world view and embrace a naturalistic point of view. The Humanist vision spread rapidly, particularly in the Midwest.

The 1933 Humanist Manifesto was written to set forth a clear summary of the Humanist worldview at a time when civilization, it was thought, was in peril. Written by philosopher Roy Wood Sellers along with Unitarian ministers Ray Bragg and Ed Wilson, it was signed by 15 Unitarians and one Universalist minister. John Dewey also signed it. Ed Wilson started a newsletter that in 1949 became the American Humanist Association. The first five presidents of the American Humanist Association were Unitarian Ministers and the AUA became the primary promoter, proselytizer and source of members. Humanist ministers were responsible for deepening Humanist thought and practice, and we attracted some of the best and brightest of the age to serve as ministers.

Humanism dramatically rescued the Unitarian Association in the nineteen fifties and sixties characterized by a liberal, progressive, intellectual elitism that was really just a continuing cultural trend dating back to the Boston Brahmins, but now increasingly dealing with real world issues. This trend was fortified by the huge growth in Fellowships which tended to be built on populations in small communities, especially college towns where the proportion of members was even more highly skewed toward the academic, intellectual pole. The joking description of "God's frozen people" had more than a sprinkling of truth.

Humanism has been built on a blend of the best of both the Enlightenment and the Romantic traditions. The marketing advantage for Unitarianism focusing on Humanism was that it had a unique identifiable brand with little ambiguity on where it stood. The *1961 UUA Preliminary Reports of the Commission of the Free Church in a Changing World* [7] concluded that with only 2.9% of UU's believing in a supernatural being and 52% believing in an explicit Humanism that the Unitarian Universalist Association should seek to build the newly merged Association on an evolving, progressive, scientific basis. It prophetically said, "Our age needs a message of liberal religion, but not the tired, unthoughtout - of mass of supercilious sophistication which piles up emptiness on emptiness – and emptiness which glibly too often passed for genuine liberalism. It needs a liberal message, but a liberal message which has been reborn, a neo-liberalism, if you please – a liberalism which has gone through the crucible of confronting the latest scientific theories.."

As the 1963 report *The Free Church in a Changing World* states, "A mind becomes mature only as its beliefs are habitually made to follow the evidence and as beliefs so formed govern both beliefs and practices. We hold that so far as it does contain beliefs it should be governed by the same earnest regard for truth and evidence as other methods of inquiry. Respect for truth should not become less as beliefs rise in scale of importance. In the first place, the use of scientific notions in theology is in keeping with our liberal traditions of rationality, of open-mindedness, of freedom of belief and conscience. Here we must give our attention to a key word in religious liberalism – truth."

The 1963 report *The Free Church in a Changing World* indeed found that the identity of the UUA was so dominated by Humanism that we should openly identify ourselves as such and build on identification with reason and science. In 1989, fully 73% of UU's identified as humanists/atheists [8]. In 1992 it was estimated to be 49% [9] and in 1997 it was 46% [10]. Today it is estimated to have declined below 40%. Most have no idea today what humanism is. Still, the vast majority of the membership today is certainly humanistic, i.e. people centered, if not actually self-identified as naturalistic Humanists.

The merger of the Unitarian and Universalist Associations was viewed with suspicion by many because of the cultural and theological differences between them. Universalism was merged as the Universalist movement was in a free fall descent at the time. Universalists, in order to stop the fall in its last days as an independent denomination, changed the message from one of universal salvation in heaven, to a message embracing all theologies universally and uncritically – radical toleration and "universal religion." Culturally there were enough differences that the merger did not blend well at first although most tried to make Universalists feel at home by extolling its rich history, and a quiet debate developed over what mutual path to take, reason in religion or radical pluralism. Radical pluralism won out, and embracing Universalism in the new formulation turned into a great marketing tool later within the Unitarian tradition for those pushing the agenda of indiscriminate pluralism. A slow process of adopting radical pluralism as the focus began. It could have gone the other way. There were indeed some Universalists like Brainard Gilbbons who asked for the Universalists to move toward rational religion and Humanism. [11] This was a lost chance as we will see.

Unitarian Universalism grew dramatically in the fifties and sixties with a focus on Humanism and in fact it became the fastest growing denomination in America peaking in 1968 at 177,431 members. [12] By 2012 the membership had diminished to 161,502. More importantly, while the population of the United States grew 54% (From 200,706,052 to 314,255,772), the UUA lost not just membership, but a percentage of market share of the population even more rapidly from 0.88% to just 0.51%. That is a 42% decrease in market share. For the fourth year in a row there has been a decline in membership. This is not just a decline, but an evaporation of membership to virtual extinction when measured by market share. Contrast this with the fact that in 1776 of those attending a church in the United States fully 70% were in Congregational churches, i.e. what are primarily now Unitarians and United Church of Christ. Along with an aging population, any market be it religion or otherwise that has declined to 0.51 % of market share in such a short time period is by definition destined for extinction. What is being done is obviously not working in building and sustaining membership. Why is this decline not a source of alarm and open examination? When one is in a congregation that is a warm loving home it may be hard to see this decline. The decline is particularly unnoticed in large suburban congregations many of which are growing. The smaller and urban congregations have seen the greatest declines, particularly the fellowships that were essentially abandoned a couple of decades ago. Another telling factor is the aging demographic mostly representing baby boomers.

In the *1967 Report on Goals*, intellectual stimulation ranked highest among congregants with respect to their reason for attending church services at 74.4%.[12] One congregation I was associated with had intellectual stimulation ranked first at 89%. The growth bubble burst in 1968 at the General Assembly in Cleveland with the dissention when the UUA gave financial support to the BAC separatist black power movement and this was protested by the integrationists in the BAWA group. Thereafter the UUA lost 7.4% of the membership in two years and 20% of the membership in ten years and never regained membership from that peak year. The UUA was almost bankrupted and destroyed with its well-meaning liberal excesses and slowly inched back some membership. We will see later how liberal excess is being replayed today.

The UUA continues to lose membership as a proportion of population. Many, including past President William Sinkford left the UUA in the 1968 debacle. More importantly, these losses came at a time when there were already great cultural stresses that played against a religion focused on reason. The counter culture that developed was a neo-romantic revolution that emphasized the experiential over the rational encompassed by the catchy slogan of the times, "Sex, drugs and rock and roll."

In the sixties, seventies, and eighties there were multiple parallel revolutions wrenching the culture such as the feminist awakening, the civil rights movement, the sexual revolution, LGBT rights revolution, popularization of pagan and nature based theologies, antiwar activism, the popularization of Eastern religions while at the same time a resurgence of fundamentalism was occurring in the general culture. Reason and rationality were not "cool" at the time. I was President of a UU congregation in the seventies and a high proportion of typical young UU's were in an open marriage or divorced, regularly smoking pot, maybe into astrology, dismissive of traditional religion, backpackers who read Kahlil Gibran, and dabbling in Buddhism, but still with Humanism as the primary grounding. Mention of God generally brought laughter. When I have said this to people who were in other congregations at that time, they say they had similar experiences with the dismissal of God talk. This experience was rather common outside of some of the more conservative Northeastern and some Southern congregations. The neo-romantic revolution cross fertilized itself in many areas. Paranormal beliefs rose greatly. As H. L. Menken said, "The curse of man and the cause of nearly all his woe, is his stupendous capacity for believing the incredible."

Credulous beliefs grew tremendously. For example, in the United States from 1976 to 1998 belief in faith healing rocketed from 10% to 45%, Astrology from 17% to 37%, Reincarnation from 9% to 25%, and Spiritualism from 12% to 52%.[14] In many cases people replaced traditional religion and science with these intensely experiential, magical modes of thinking. As Carl Sagan said, "If it were widely understood that claims to knowledge require adequate evidence before they can be accepted, there would be no room for pseudoscience. But a kind of Gresham's Law prevails in popular culture by which bad science drives out good." [15]

The turning away from the Enlightenment project was in some ways part of an old American tradition. As Richard Hofstadter observed in *Anti-Intellectualism in American Life*, "Intellect in America is resented as a kind of excellence, as a claim to distinction, as a challenge to egalitarianism, as a quality which almost certainly deprives a man or woman of the common touch." [16] Radical egalitarianism eventually won out.

Let's look closer now at a few of the primary historical, intellectual, and cultural changes that have affected the UUA's evolution before drawing these trends together.

Unbalanced Humanism

D URING THE SEVENTIES, Paul Kurtz was the editor of the Humanist magazine, the publication arm of the American Humanist Association. Paul was a brilliant student of Sidney Hook who in turn was a student of John Dewey. Intellectually devoted to pragmatism and a balanced humanism he, by temperament, was more inclined to the rational pole rather than the emotional pole of humanism. He had been a UU, but became distraught over the theistic growth and, more important, the irrational tendencies that were just developing. At the same time he was concerned by the New Age pseudoscience and increasing influence of irrationalism in the general culture. He placed a great deal of emphasis on critical reasoning and started the skeptical movement with the Skeptical Inquirer magazine. He left the AHA when he demanded total financial control, was turned down, and then started what would eventually become the Council for Secular Humanism. He distinguished between religious and secular humanism more for market branding than for ideological reasons. Regardless, he bent the humanist movement away from emotional, evocative, communitarian ideals towards rationalistic, critical thinking and religious criticism; an unbalanced humanism.

Many during this period many were critical of over rationalism in the UUA and blamed humanism specifically. An example would be the "talk backs" after a sermon that many times degenerated without proper monitoring into dispiriting arguing usually by a few dominating misanthropic people. The proper balance of religious criticism versus religious tolerance is hard to determine and manage. Good arguments can be made for both extremes. Still, as Rev. Suzanne Paul, a Humanist minister serving UU churches says, "The UUA could not figure out - nor did they have the courage - to call these people out for their bad behavior. So they have taken what I see as the coward's way out - they have created a denomination that no longer appeals to Humanists - but in so doing - they gave Humanism away. They wanted to shoot the messengers, not the message. "

With the cultural trends away from reason and science, the stereotyping of humanists as "angry old white men", humanism was viewed as passé and destructive to the UUA. The Humanists who forgot to honor the experiential and compassionate reinforced the image of humanists as head only rationalists. The stereotype did not honor the majority of balanced Humanists. Still, it is curious to see how the cultural trends in society at large are now back toward Humanism and the UUA is largely paralyzed in knowing where to turn now.

11

Postmodernism and the Death of Reason

THE ACADEMIC PHILOSOPHY of Postmodernism took a huge toll on Western culture in the last quarter of the twentieth century. Postmodernism premises that all we know is a social construction, and both the Enlightenment and the Romantic projects are merely tools used to rationalize power and control over others. Postmodernism is an extreme form of subjectivism and skepticism that took over academia, the UU ministry and subtly within general culture. Many ministers and lay people adhere to it without even knowing of its ideological basis, but are biased toward its relativism and anti-intellectualism. You can hear it in every day phrases like, "One belief is as good as another", "Who am I to judge?", and, "It's all relative."

Postmodernism has been discredited, is on the wane, and even its most ardent followers are disavowing it. While it frequently has provided good insights especially into the domination of minorities, its basis in total relativism has bolstered the overall relativistic direction in the UUA whose cognitive emptiness can seem to be intellectually rationalized. As Richard Evans says, "Of course it is right to say that we can never know the whole or absolute truth about anything in the past. But, just because we can never attain the whole or absolute truth, just because we make mistakes in our search for the truth about the past, just because there will always be something new to say about any historical subject, it does not follow that there is no such thing as the truth at all." [17]

UU's like to think they are on the cutting edge, but in fact seem to always trail the real edge of thinking and the continued adherence to Postmodern epistemology is a good example. Postmodernism has been termed *Fashionable Nonsense* from the book by that title by Alan Sokal and Jean Bricmont which exposed its hollowness. [18] Postmodernism academically is quickly decaying, but its pernicious effects linger throughout academia and within the UUA. Even one of the greatest exponents, Terry Eagleton, who wrote the Postmodern classic *Literary Theory* [19] recently wrote a refutation titled *After Theory* [20]. He saw he was going to be on the wrong side of history and rushed to the exit.

Unitarian Universalism is still enmeshed in a relativist postmodern culture that oozes its nihilistic poison throughout the association. The *2005 Commission on Appraisal* report says, "Postmodern critiques do affirm that attention to our particularity comes closer to what is real than concepts of a unified reality." [21] Read that as saying that our focus should be on individual experience rather than overarching foundations for truth and meaning which we can't believe in anymore. Postmodern relativism is uncritically and broadly accepted as the truth (oddly because there isn't supposed to be any) within the leadership of the UUA. Recent attempts to discard the fourth principle, "A free and responsible search for truth and meaning", and the source of "Humanist teachings which counsel us to heed the guidance of reason and the results of science, and warn us against idolatries of the mind and spirit" tell us that the search for truth has been discarded as well as the humanist heritage. Postmodern ideology is a poisoned chalice for any real liberalism.

Second Wave Academic Feminists and Further Epistemological Suicide

THE UNITARIAN UNIVERSALIST Association was an early and ardent supporter of women's rights and the broader goal of changing our culture to equalize the treatment of women. A wonderful, Feminist revolution rose that expanded our consciousness and created long overdue changes. A curious thing happened on the academic front though. Second wave academic feminism, borrowing from Postmodernism, became dominated by the ideas that reason and science were only male tools for power and control and thus to be discounted. Books like *Woman, Knowledge and Reality* [22] were broadly used in academia to justify the notion that women's thinking was better than men's as they used intuitional skills to determine truth while men were "head only", noncompassionate Rationalists. Woman's studies denounced objective knowledge and rationality as so much "male oppression." This epistemological dogma spread rapidly. Those in disagreement with this epistemology were marginalized out of the feminist club of intuitional true believers. Meanwhile, Feminism made great strides within the UUA by the

15

fact that the number of woman in the ministry at the end of the twentieth century increased dramatically to 53% today.

While all of us applaud the cultural Feminist revolution expanding woman's rights and exposing male hierarchy, to many the attack on the Enlightenment project was disconcerting. There were a few women who stood up to this disparagement of reason and science such as Susan Jacoby in *The Age of American Unreason* [23], and Camille Paglia who calls it mostly "pretentious nonsense." Still, as the Rev. Kendyl Gibbons cautioned, "The first chapter of the Enlightenment may be closed, but reason and objective truth, like Pauline of the Perils, has a way of making a comeback out of seemingly dire situations." It has. The UUA in many venues seems still stuck in second wave feminism while the general culture and certainly the feminist movement at large has moved on to third wave feminism that does not disparage reason, especially amongst the Millennial generation. Many of the young third wave feminists such as Greta Christina are very science oriented and feel second wave feminism has set the overall feminist movement back.

The culture changed in the UUA from one extolling the use of reason in religion to one openly disparaging and hostile to reason and subsequently hostile to Humanism. A minister's conference was held in the late 90's in Hot Springs, Arkansas, to develop a definition of the UUA for a new millennium. Theists dominated the conference and when an amendment to honor reason in religion was introduced in a consensus statement, a whole day of bitter rancor resulted with strong rhetoric against reason, and the conference closed without adopting the statement. It was then I knew that the tide had turned irreversibly especially after one pagan minister laughingly told a Humanist minister that they just needed to wait until all the Humanists died to take over. Tellingly, the 2007 *Leaping From Our Spheres* analysis of the impact of woman on the Unitarian Universalist Ministry questioning ministers on sources of authority did not even include reason or science in the list on the questionnaire even though 56% of woman ministers claimed to be Atheists or Humanists in the study. [24] A deep Epistemological fracture still exists.

New Age – Old Wine in New Skins

ANOTHER POPULAR FASHION has been the New Age mixture of gullible neo-romantic and pseudoscientific beliefs. Ironically some of it originally stemmed from the human potential movement and humanists such as Eric Fromm, Abraham Maslow, and Carl Rogers, but has morphed into an overblown utopian idealism about the potentialities of human nature. Culturally and intellectually it has credulously embraced every kind of magical thinking from Homeopathy, Astrology, energy fields, angels, ESP, Qigong, and an infinite variety of other optimistic irrational beliefs. As Susan Jacoby says, "This mindless tolerance, which places observable scientific facts, subject to proof, on the same level as unprovable supernatural fantasy, has played a major role in the resurgence of both anti-intellectualism and anti-rationalism." [25] William Ellery Channing once said, "Believe in the power of truth and love." He would be surprised that belief in truth had been so callously dismissed.

As one person said to me, "All my friends gave up the old religions only to embrace a whole lot of new trendy bull." Things like this aren't supposed to be said in polite, tolerant, uncritical UU society, but I think we need to say directly what the unvarnished problems are here, as they are too often swept under the carpet within the culture. Much of this irrational thinking is a result of epistemological ignorance.

18

Either one tends to see knowledge in terms of an empirical, scientific worldview based on facts, or see it based in terms of fanciful optimism based on ungrounded feelings. Much of these faith-based beliefs are merely the result of intellectual laziness.

You can, as the saying goes, "Open your mind so wide your brains fall out." Scientific critical thinking and ungrounded irrational methodologies are incommensurable world views which have resulted in much tension in recent years. The responsible search for truth has been replaced by an ideology of toleration and diversity whereby critical voices have been silenced and smiling politeness masks the ugliness of a toxic retreat to a neo-romantic utopianism. Euripides' dictum that "Humanity's most valuable trait is a judicious sense of what not to believe" appears to have been forgotten.

Theological Professors Justify Their Jobs and the Religious Culture Shifts

Within the theological schools there was a significant revolution beginning with Paul Tillich's book *The Courage to Be* [26] in which he suggested we could redefine the word God in secular terms as "that which is our ultimate concern." This concept of looking at religion from its functional aspects has a long history. In 1873 Felix Adler had returned from neo-Kantian Rabbinical studies in Germany to give an address that eventually was used to found the Ethical Society based on the idea that religion is not based on theology, but in practice on community and ethics. [27]

Anthropologists, sociologists, psychologists and later evolutionary psychologist scholars saw that the religious impulses were exhibited and practiced in a number of consistent ways across cultures and religions beyond belief systems such as the use of totems, ritual, ethical standards, the binding of community and children's education. I make a distinction between the religious impulses and religion in this paper. Many times in academia the term religion is used in the functional sense pointing to the non-ideological, non-supernatural aspects where the beliefs and practices sustain the foundations we live by. Academics look broadly at religion trying to understand how the religious impulses are played out in practice.

Religious impulses should be seen as not the purveyance of religion, but instinctual impulses of our core humanity. Religions have sold the idea that these impulses are only answered by religion. They certainly "empower" religion, but they are our humanity speaking on a wide variety of primal drives.

The science of Evolutionary Psychology has exploded on the scene in recent years giving insights into human motivations, instincts, drives, and impulses. Regarding religion, the science is only beginning to uncover the source of religious drive. In fact, there is considerable ongoing controversy about whether religion itself is a separate evolutionary adaptive trait, or whether religion represents the result of a number of adaptive traits such as tribalism, other worldliness, ritualism, self-reflective consciousness, status driven power "tribal" leadership, binding morality, and fear of death. All of these on their own are well known evolutionary adaptive traits to help us survive and reproduce.

We need not get bogged down in the subtleties of evolutionary psychology debates. It is enough merely to know that each of the impulses are natural impulses exhibited in all of us. The difference is that the secular person looks at these impulses and sees no need for supernatural, religious or non-scientific explanations. The secular person sees that some of these impulses should be understood and promoted such as needs for community, binding moralities, understandings of our origins and death, of our needs for awe and wonder, our needs for purpose, and in some cases, our needs for rituals. But we can discriminate and reject those impulses that don't serve us well today such as tribalism, needs for power and control, male dominance, other worldliness, authoritarian figures or beliefs, magic beliefs, and harmful rituals. Biology is not destiny.

For Humanists, we can indeed hold onto and modify those impulses that fortify religion and can enhance the secular life, but we need not call them religious as they are indeed part of what makes us human. Religion has no monopoly on needs for community, ritual, rites of passage, uncovering a whole worldview, building an ethical life, searching for meaning and purpose, seeking emotional transcendence, and embracing awe and wonder.

That is why I think the term "Religious" Humanism needs to be discarded at this point in our historical, intellectual, linguistic, and cultural evolution. It's time to move on. I prefer not using any adjectives before describing my Humanism be it religious, ethical, or secular. Just say you are a Humanist. I have travelled widely in Humanist circles and have found that there is little difference between all the different "styles" and no matter how seculars describe themselves be it Humanist, Atheist, Freethinker etc. as most agree on 95% of all beliefs and more important values. Quibbling about if their style, if more rational or experiential, more communitarian or solitary, more anti-religion or more tolerant of religion is fruitless as we all gravitate toward some style or emphasis that may fit us better than others or we may even change our own style during the day.

In general usage, the words religion and God almost always points toward supernatural beliefs and practices and we should normally use them in this way. (Miriam Webster first definition – "the service and worship of God or the supernatural") But in UU circles the word God has become an all-purpose enigmatic metaphor. It has become a piety widget. John Dewey envisioned that it would be best to have the culture turn from theism to Humanism in a slow evolutionary change rather than a quick revolutionary one. In his book *A*

Common Faith he initially thought that one tool to accomplish this would be to use traditional religious words metaphorically and introduced a distinction between "religion" and the "religious" for a transition period. [28] He quickly learned that theists would misinterpret this metaphorical distinction or use it as a weapon against Humanism and later he regretted using religious words metaphorically and functionally. This early experience in religious redefinition should have been a warning for what has happened today.

In theological schools the secular revolution had a deep impact. In 1961 the book, *The Death of God* by Gabriel Vahanian helped define the growing Death of God movement. [29] Many professors in mainstream theological schools embraced the death of God movement such as the Christian theologians Gabriel Vahanian, Paul Van Buren, William Hamilton, Thomas J. J. Altizer, and the rabbi Richard L. Rubenstein culminating in the famous April 8, 1966 *Time* magazine cover proclaiming the death of God.

The tide had turned in history or so it seemed to others and myself at the time. These theologians pushed the limits of what was to be tolerated in theological schools, and they paid a heavy price as every one of the main characters in the Death of God movement were pushed out of their positions. The message became clear in theological schools that one could be a doubter, an agnostic, or even a complete atheist, but keep it quiet and couch your words in religious language relying on metaphor to keep your job. "Theological professorships are pretty good jobs" as the Dean of a prominent Christian theological school put it after admitting he was a closet Humanist to me. With candor and a knowing smile he said, "I've got too much invested in my position now to blow it." Follow the money to understand these things.

Countless solutions to the secular problem were created in theological schools such as Wilfred Cantwell Smith's redefinition of God as, "that in which we have faith", or "that on which we ultimately rely". These ideas do contain an elegant psychological truth imbedded within, but still ignore the traditional supernatural basis of religion. Rem Edwards has a very sophisticated analysis of the word religion using Ludwig Wittgenstein's "family traits" analysis that illustrates the lack of functional definitional boundaries of the word religion where even golf could be considered a religion to some. [30] This why we need to use a clear ideological definition in normal conversation.

No solution to the problem of secularization within Theological Schools was as successful as Process Theology that originally developed out of ideas by the philosopher Alfred North Whitehead, but given real voice by Charles Hartshorne, John B. Cobb, Jr., and David Ray Griffin. [31] In recent years a number of prominent Jewish theologians and public intellectuals such as William E. Kaufman, Harold Kushner, Anton Laytner, and Michael Lerner have embraced process theology. Hartshorne postulated a Panentheism (all is in God) that must be differentiated from Pantheism (all is God).

This muddle of words and enigmatic distinctions was given more credence at Meadville Lombard Theological School and the UUA in general by the process theologian Ralph Wendell Burhoe who conflated religion and science. Still, Ralph Burhoe teamed with the Humanist Robert Tapp and founded the magazine Zygon to promote the scientific thinking of religion. Today it is published out of a Lutheran seminary and caters to Process Theology.

The billionaire financier John Templeton became enamored with Process Theology and set up an annual "Templeton Prize for Progress Toward Research or Discoveries about Spiritual Realities" whose annual prize is larger than the Nobel Prize. The fight for the prize money in theological schools has managed to legitimize the idea that supernatural theological ideas have a scientific basis. But note the title of the prize, which presupposes the premise that there actually are spiritual realities. Again, follow the money - really, really big money - 2.3 billion dollars in the fund this year. This mouthwatering financial carrot has influenced all theological schools and theology in general.

Process Theology is only one part of a whole theological shift from the identifiable personal God of Abrahamic religions to the variety of vague notions of God we have today. We now have the Process Theological God who is part of all that is, but not quite Pantheistic. We also have the "God of the Gaps" because some are uncomfortable with their own ignorance. The fact is that science keeps shrinking the unknown and the world becomes increasingly knowable. It is telling that this unexplained mystery is always spoken of in hushed tones. The so-called, "God of the Gaps" keeps shrinking and is increasingly intellectually untenable. As Einstein said, "The most incomprehensible thing about the universe is that it is comprehensible."

The UUA has tried to capitalize on a wealth of studies regarding modern religious orientation toward the self. As Kosmin and Lackman have shown, religion for most is but a thin veneer over what is really a pragmatic secular life. [32] Harold Bloom in *The American Religion* sees American religion as unique in embodying a Gnosticism centered on personal experience. "The God of American religion is an experiential God, so radically within our own being as to become a virtual identity with what is most authentic (oldest and best) in the self." [33] As R. Lawrence Moore in *Selling God* points out, religion in America is a commodity of the self. Traditional notions of God are being redefined by all. [34] The center does not hold in any religious tradition as we hear the words "preference" and "opinion" replacing traditionalism and dogmatism in this world of postmodern self-referential relativism.

Entering the twenty first century we see an America where, "Boundaries separating one faith tradition from another that once seemed fixed are now often blurred; religious identifications are malleable and multifaceted, often overlapping several traditions." [35] People have learned to embrace and syncretize many different religious beliefs and practices. Traditional religion and particularly institutional religion continues to lose influence while at the same time individualistic religion dominates.

Ultimate authority for religious meaning and truth come today not from institutional authority, science, and reason, but from inner existential and experiential voices. The locus of meaning has been driven into the well of direct experience and the authority of individualism. In many cases the Emersonian transcendental urge is fulfilled with an image of a God of immanence within oneself. It has to do more with feelings and awareness that are authentic only to the individual. Religion, always a meaning-making story, is only authentic today if it is our story. The "sacred" is that which is sacred only to us. For religion to be true and meaningful it must emanate from our own experiences. This emphasis of religion is termed "Sheilaism" in Robert Bellah's book *Habits of the Heart* after a woman who exemplified this trend. [36]

We now have a generalized, syncretized, enigmatic "fuzzy theism" which is intuitional, variable and individualized and yet having similar attributes in some regards. It is a "God" who adapts to the situation, sometimes merely an "energy" in the universe, sometimes morphing into the creator God, sometimes framed in terms of the indeterminacy of Quantum mechanics, and mostly having the uplifting characteristics of American optimism and reassurance.

It is never an intellectually reflective theology as much as a purely experiential one. When Oprah Winfrey sells a religious outlook you know it will have mass appeal. The mantra today is, "I'm not religious; I'm spiritual" (INRIS) keeping it just vague enough to not offend others while providing an image of moral piousness. The word spirituality sells well because it is a Rorschach test for everyone's view of what is emotionally important to them, but in the end neither informs nor communicates, and most important, skews religion toward a God of everlasting inwardness.

These trends continue today, but probably not for long. The religion of self referentiality is already showing the wear and loss of its own destructive nihilistic seeds. The question is if the UUA will continue trying to market to this baby boomer dominated trend and find itself behind the marketing curve again.

He Who Controls the Language
Controls the Debate

UNITARIAN UNIVERSALIST MINISTERS have tried to capitalize on these trends by becoming masters of the religious redefinition game. When Humanism was dominant there was too much emphasis by some toward a Platonic rigidity in the use of words. Many were fearful of any metaphors and, more important, of any religious language as many were angry "come-outers" from religion. Others saw the revival and use of religious metaphoric language as crucial to the UUA. Some saw it as a way to revitalize theism or at least to make theists feel welcome.

Ministers in the latter camp used the argument on one hand that we can't let the fundamentalists have all the good words, or alternatively that Humanists need not be afraid of words, and implemented a concerted effort to reintroduce religious language. The result of this is that many Humanists felt uncomfortable and consequently many left rather than compromise their intellectual and religious integrity with what they saw as a regressive, conservative direction. Those who did not conform were labeled as unsophisticated about religion, intolerant, angry at God, or "fundamentalist" Humanists. While the argument was and still is that the UUA is trying to merely seek evocative, poetic language that all could use, the reality is that traditional religious language fosters the conservative theistic directions that have marginalized Humanists, and that naturalistic and supernatural language remains largely incommensurable.

One is reminded of *Alice in Wonderland*. "When I use a word," Humpty Dumpty said, in rather a scornful tone, "it means just what I choose it to mean—neither more nor less." "The question is," said Alice, "whether you can make words mean so many different things." "The question is," said Humpty Dumpty, " which is to be master—that's all." We now know who the masters are.

The greatest creativity shown by UUA ministers today is in writing sermons with new and innovative ways of playing the religious redefinition game whereby words like God, spirit, soul, prayer, sin, worship, sacred, religion, faith, and holy are incorporated trying to make them amenable to all. Importantly, the context is kept enigmatic and Humanists are asked (demanded?) to redefine religious language in naturalistic ways when the context clearly demands a supernatural basis. I am unable to comprehend a non-supernatural frame of reference for the word pray. The late Reverend Forrester Church was masterful in this technique which ultimately has not fostered a widened theological diversity as much is it has pushed out Humanists and focused the UUA even more on the "Fuzzy Theist", New Age, Process Theological position. In fact, it could be argued that today this is the de facto theological position in the UUA.

One of the most destructive obfuscations is of the word faith. There are two completely different definitions, one of faith being ungrounded belief and indeed belief in something in spite of the facts. The other is a synonym for reliance. We all rely on things, but as a humanist I choose to rely on well-grounded belief. Reliance on ungrounded faith based belief is one of the greatest dangers to our civilization and the cause of much of our woes. When the UU conflates the two definitions and fails to distinguish between them it is complicit in supporting the modern dark ages.

Congregants start to think that language obfuscation is enlightened religion, but in fact it has become just a tool to manipulate the congregants toward a particular view. As the 18th century philosopher William Hazlitt spoke of the late Mr. Pitt, "The fog and haze in which he saw everything communicated itself to others; and the total indistinctness and uncertainty of his own ideas tended to confound the perceptions of his hearers more effectually than the most ingenious misrepresentation could have done."

There is another view. It is that language serves as our most important tool for communication and sharing knowledge. Beyond being a pragmatic communication tool, language is also an elegant paintbrush to reveal our inner humanity.

One can acknowledge that some may find a homogenized religion avowing the hazy metaphor of the "Spirit of Life" or "Universal Spirit" as meaningful and evocative, but most do not and eventually drift to clearer language. One does not have to be "angry about religion" or close minded to find this type of supernatural language politically laden, evasive, manipulative, meaningless, and boring. The religious language redefinition game may harbor deep metaphoric meanings for some, but for others the distance between theist and non-theist worldviews are insurmountable, and that is all right. A deep pluralism acknowledges we will have these irresolvable differences and will deal with them with no utopian dreams of universal understanding, language, or basis for community.

Early on the Rev. Mark Belletini found that the definitions of spirituality had become so diverse, contradictory, and incommensurable, that maybe we should, as liberals, give this word a moratorium. It has now become too forced, loaded and is an impediment to healthy communication. Religious language has become a manipulative tool that allows us to pretend we are all talking about the same things when in fact there are irresolvable differences. It uses such broad-based metaphors that it prevents us from really saying what we mean when using specific language would be far better. For example, rather than "spiritual" it might be better to be specific and say, "my feelings of wholeness and purpose", or "that which emotionally uplifts me", or "that which is transcendent to me," or "God talks to me and fills me with love" etc., whatever is the true meaning we want to get across. We need to stop pretending we are all talking about the same thing when we use the word spiritual. Generally we are not.

Henry Hitchings documents the larger battle in his recent book, *The Language Wars* [37] that was being fought long before the UUA entered the fray. He separates the battle lines between the Prescriptivists who use reason and logic to adjust our definitions, and the Descriptivists who "saw language as a complicated jungle of habits that it would be impossible to trim into shape." The UUA appears to have embraced an extreme Descriptivist point of view. Joseph Epstein's position is that "language is mutable, but reserves the right to loathe certain changes; however widely accepted they may be." [38] I would count the words God, faith, and religion in that category. The issue is deeper though.

There is an ethics of words. It requires us to be honest with our language and to bear responsibility that our communication is not misunderstood. It requires that we know when and where to use metaphor and when to use specific descriptive language and to responsibly insure that the listener understands what we really mean. God is a perfectly good word for belief in a personal supernatural being and is what most people normally use. God can be a great metaphor as well, but not in the flippant manner it is used in UUA pulpits today.

In academia the word religion can be used in more relative functional terms always remembering to provide people with the definition you are using at the time, but for common language we are almost always taking about practices relating to supernatural beliefs and commitments. Let us forget the word spirituality for now - it needs a break not because it doesn't mean anything, but it means too much. Determine the specifics of what you really mean and communicate it without obfuscation to the listener. We owe them that honor.

As George Orwell said, "But if thought corrupts language, language can also corrupt thought." And the corruption of a language and thought is exactly what we have seen. "Distortive language", George Orwell wrote in 1946, "was not to express meanings as to destroy them." Words could be destroyed by wantonly expanding their terms so that they came completely to replace a whole range of older, more specific, and more definitive terms and usage's.

Richard Dawkins in a lecture to the AHA provided two rules for the use of metaphors. One, they must do real explanatory work and, two, they should be identifiable as a metaphor.

Yes, we need metaphor, but the purposeful distortion in clear communication has degraded our personal, interpersonal, and intellectual growth. We would do better to have more courage and clarity in our communication. Say what you mean, and mean what you say.

Humanism and its Enemies

I T IS UNEQUIVOCAL that Humanism was deliberately and purposely pushed out of the UUA. Lest one think this is a radical, paranoid statement let us look at the facts. President Bill Schultz, a Humanist who wrote his doctoral thesis on the development of Humanist Manifesto I, rightly sought to temper some of the worst rationalistic, anti-ritual tendencies of the time, but President John Buehrens purposefully sought to instill theism back into the UUA. In the first edition of his book *A Common Faith* co-authored with F. Forrester Church they said, "Even as the Humanist Manifesto was being drafted, in Nazi Germany the sponsors of another 'vital movement in the direction of a candid and explicit humanism' were beginning to spin a web of horror that would ensnare, desecrate, and massacre life in the most blasphemous way: genocide." [39]

It's hard to even imagine a more hateful and demonizing statement when Humanism is linked with Nazism and genocide. After other Humanists and I repeatedly objected, Buehrens and Church reluctantly took the statement out of later editions.

The irony is that this follows an early Postmodern myth developed by Marxists Max Horkmeimer and Theodor Adorno in their book, "Dialectic of Enlightenment" [40] to rationalize why Marxism had led to the deaths of thirty million people under Stalin. Of course they couldn't blame Marxism so they blamed the Enlightenment, reason, Modernism and Humanism. Many have fallen for this destructive excuse from the real cause, totalitarian Marxism itself, and this trope continues today. Buehrens and Church fell into the Marxists intellectual trap and appear to have used it quite happily as a rationalization for their own anti-humanist beliefs.

President William Sinkford accelerated the reinstitution of a focus on theism and the rejection of Humanism. Once an ardent Humanist, he left the church during the Black Power conflict in the late sixties and later had a theistic religious conversion. He was recruited back into the UUA and, in order to demonstrate the UUA commitment to racial justice, he immediately was recruited for the Presidency despite the fact that he had virtually no ministerial experience. In personal conversations with him he could barely contain his disdain for Humanism.

When the Boy Scouts sought to bar all who would not sign a pledge of belief in God, I was involved at a national level as President of the American Humanist Association (AHA) to defend non-believers and hoped that the UUA would join as well. President Sinkford's initial statement was tepid support for Humanists at best, but he then initiated a debate about LGBT discrimination issues, which were an additional problem as well with the Boy Scouts, but not the immediate one at hand. I watched as the public statements then evolved to only defending LGBT issues and any defense of Humanism went silent. His silence told volumes. Many Humanists feel that the ministers pulled the laity toward a fuzzy theism and away from Humanism, not the other way around. Today one can viscerally feel the contempt and fear of Humanism when talking to many UU ministers especially when they find it hard to use the word Humanist without the word fundamentalist before it. Luckily there are many who still unapologetically defend Humanism.

In their recent 2010 book *Liberal Religion is Not Just a Compromise* John Buehrens and Starr King School for the Ministry President Rebecca Ann Parker double down on their vision of a "tide of progressive religion rising" seeing Postmodernism, moving to the middle theologically, and focusing on liberal progressive politics as their marketing plan. All of this is despite all empirical evidence that this marketing plan is failing. [41] Few dare disagree.

But, there are a few notable dissenting voices. The Rev. Robert Latham in his essay *Does Unitarian Universalism Have a Future* points out that "institutions succeed to the extent they effectively fulfill their mission," and instead of a mission we substituted community, social action and political correctness, and the end result is a persistent identity crisis. Devotion to diversity as a grounding principle ...points us toward chaos and gives priority to individual need." [42]

Latham also says that, "To become such a unified and transformative religious community we must overcome the fear of our primal nemesis. This nemesis is the notion that if we hold a common answer to anything profound we will have created a dogma like the religious right."

Meadville Lombard professor Rev. David Bumbaugh in his paper, *The Marketing of Liberal Religion* [43] rightly says, "Liberal Religion faces the possibility that it may be overwhelmed by an ... ambient spirituality that has no outward focus but slides easily into a therapeutic mode, offering an endless journey of infinite regression into the self." "They offer an unexamined piety rather than a solid faith." And the

UUA is now "...an institution offering therapy rather than faith, comfort rather than adventure." He warns that "the refusal to embrace a clear identity threatens to sweep Liberal Religion into a commodified, thumbsucking irrelevance."

These courageous and insightful words seem to have had little effect on an entrenched bureaucracy wedded to the dumbed down, therapeutic religious model, a clergy afraid to challenge them, and a laity ignorant that their leaders have destroyed the best of what liberal religion can promise.

Theological Education

MOST THEOLOGICAL STUDENTS gradually learn and embrace a pragmatic idea of the function of ministry. With fifty percent of ministers in all denominations not continuing after their first placement it is no wonder that ministers are told to not let theology get in the way of pastoral success. If you have to, talk down to the laity as they are just not sophisticated enough to understand Postmodernism, Process Theology and such. The message is clear that if you want to have a job as a minister in any denomination, place the emphasis of your ministry on placating the parishioners and keeping the peace. Follow the money.

Our institutional memory and a coherent ministerial education have been lost in recent years with the loss of denominational ministerial schools. At Harvard Theological School the loss of James Luther Adams, George Huston Williams and Conrad Wright as the last major Unitarian presence was a large enough blow, but Harvard, once the bastion of secular religion, turned away from any Humanist leanings in recent years. Even Harvey Cox the author of *The Secular City* reading the direction of the conservative winds has gone back and embraced a more theistic, even evangelical tone. As one UUA graduate put it, "At Harvard they totally embrace every kind of weird religion, but don't call yourself a Humanist as that is the bogey man all can rail against."

At Starr King School for the Ministry a major shift came when Rebecca Parker, a gifted Methodist minister, was appointed in 1990 to be the President. Under President Parker's leadership the focus became more on religion as liberal politics and ministers as wounded healers. Foundational religion became irrelevant and anti-oppression politics, gender identity, therapeutic religion, and other forms of liberal activism now dominate the agenda. Identity politics replaced academic inquiry. Academia has betrayed its overall purpose and open intellectual inquiry has been replaced by ideological indoctrination.

Dr. Parker's personal ministerial gospel spoke to the mission of ministry as wounded healers based on the assumption that all of us are damaged, wounded souls and our ministry and communities should provide supportive nurturing to shattered and damaged lives. Religious considerations are unimportant in this world-view, and it offers a liberal religion that is more like supportive therapy especially around issues related to gender identity. In a comment made to a Humanist friend of mine, Parker said, "I am still learning how to be a Christian."

There is another model that has been superseded by the therapeutic, wounded healer model of the ministry. It is the Prophetic, heroic ministry model. Within the Old Testament there are the Prophetic and the Priestly models of ministry. The Priestly, conservative, feel good, therapeutic model maintains the ministry and status quo, while the Prophetic, heroic tradition challenges us to greater heights understanding it is only in conflict that we can change and grow as none of us want to change and must be challenged to do so.

James O. Prochaska and Carlo C. DiClemente [44] have developed a meta-theory of change after observing how people change on any issue. In it, there are predictable stages of change for any growth and each stage must involve some discomfort. Without challenge we remain where we are. We are inherently conservative creatures, which is why a feel good, non-confrontational religion, while comforting, keeps us right where we are, and we fail to change and grow and work out our problems.

Emerson with his self-reliance model was a heroic model as is Humanism, where one is expected to fully realize one's potential despite many hurdles in our path. The pantheon of past heroes like Michael Servetus, Joseph Priestly, William Ellery Channing, Hosea Ballou, Ralph Waldo Emerson, Theodore Parker, John Murray and John Dietrich were all unapologetic prophetic voices of their age. The therapeutic model is essential in times of strife, but pandering to every belief uncritically ultimately disempowers the laity, muzzles the ministers, and increases dependence on the group. In fact the 1997 report by the Commission on Appraisal in fact is titled *Interdependence*. There needs to be a dialectical balance between the two models, but the Priestly model totally dominates today. Egalitarianism has won out over elitism; dependency over Emersonian self-reliance. Soothing words have replaced challenging thought. Supportive words are prized over critical intelligence.

In addition, most ministers today have abandoned their rabbinical duty toward education and intellectual excellence. The rabbinical ethical and educational duty is to help people gain foundations for the good life. Even in children's education there is little but the constant drumbeat of tolerance taught. If providing grounding for life is an ethical imperative then the UUA has failed both its adults and its children badly. Personally, I am appalled when I see so many rootless children and the rootlessness of their lives. If UU's have a stain on their conscience, it is our abject failure of responsibility to the children in helping them forge a realistic and bountiful grounding in life. Postmodernism tells us we have nothing to teach each other because there are no real foundations for any belief and the result is the damage to our children's lives. Hodding Carter is famously quoted saying, "There are only two lasting bequests we can hope to give our children. One of these is roots, the other, wings." We do great on the wings, but our children are left to fly direction-less which is possibly why the UUA has the lowest retention ratio of any denomination at only 12%.

Possibly more important, the decline in skills in epistemology, science, and overall critical thinking have degraded the ministry to a point where most do not have enough of a foundation to teach much of anything other than watered down theology, liberal politics, and pop psychology. Although one sees many ministers intellectually challenging themselves and their congregations, one also sees a lot of bad poetry being generated and emotional manipulation is a well-developed skill amongst many in the ministry. Services promising "spirituality" many times descend to vacuous stagecraft.

Meadville Lombard has always been the primary Unitarian theological school and indeed has shown to have the greatest overall success in developing ministers in the Association. Humanism had a strong presence there in the forties, fifties, sixties and seventies. It was not always so. Edwin H. Wilson, the founder of the American Humanist Association, loved to tell the story of walking up the steps of the school his first day in 1922 (When the school was still in Pennsylvania) and meeting two departing students hauling their bags out the door. When asked why they were leaving they replied that they had openly admitted they were humanists and were thrown out for it. Ed did not know what Humanism was at the time, but decided he would find out since it seemed so controversial, and so began his journey as one of the greatest promoters of Humanism and founder of the American Humanist Association (AHA).

Today Humanism is a mere whisper of itself at Meadville Lombard and for years students have been discouraged from identifying themselves as Humanists. One student admitted to me that he was a Humanist, but said he was going to keep it quiet. He was applying for settlement and pronounced he would be anything any congregation wanted him to be. He validated Marx's theory that economic considerations precede and determine religion, not the other way around. Marx knew. Follow the money.

However, in 2000 Meadville Lombard began offering a course in "Religious Humanism" taught first by the Rev. Dr. Carol Hepokoski and more recently by the Rev. Dr. William Murry. The course has been popular with both Humanist students and students seeking to learn about Humanism. Unfortunately that course has now been dropped from the curriculum.

Meadville Lombard's recent financial crises and initial decision to merge with Andover Newton Theological School (ANTS) was particularly troubling. Meadville had determined it was in their best interests, and they could remain independent at least for now. Following through on the merger the UUA would have lost any denominational, intellectual, cultural, and institutional focus and would have become yet another liberal Christian religion without any distinctive voice or as they say in business, market brand. Former Meadville Lombard professor Dr. Robert Tapp sees it as a regression to the mean. As Gretchen Robinson, a Humanist and recent graduate of Andover Newton put it, "Christian and Jewish thought... imbued every workshop. The students talked about God as if he exists and controls human life. Not once in my time there did anyone use the word "humanist" (other than "Christian humanist"). Nor was space ever made for a humanist perspective. ANTS president, Rev. Nick Carter, is a charismatic and energetic man, committed to the welfare of humankind. He is also a committed Christian. ... I know they are all committed to 'The Great Commission,' Jesus' instructions to 'go forth and convert the nations.' "

Currently Meadville Lombard has elected to move into the space of a Jewish theological school, and this will result in the UUA identify becoming less identifiable. The merging of the libraries will render the excellent humanist literature and history at significant risk. Thankfully there are efforts to save it, but the natural process over time will not protect our important literary heritage. Particularly distressing is the lack of an academic seriousness as pastoral education becomes more dominant. The whole program has moved away from a multiyear residential academic program toward short intensives and online education. Meadville Lombard is becoming more like an online trade school than an academic program. The UUA identification as a separate prophetic voice is further diluted and our movement continues its unhampered march to the theological right.

The danger is that the UUA institutional memory could be erased and forgotten as it already has at Harvard. Unitarianism for most of its history had a uniquely positioned market "brand" of rational religion. It grew as culture was progressively rejecting faith based religion, but now moves backward toward a mediocre middle position that is dying. As Brian Wilson of the Beach Boys said, "Beware the lollipop of mediocrity. Lick once and you suck forever." The utopian dream by some in the UUA is that we can become the unifying religion for all by widening the market and moving to a more conservative religious stance. The reality is that it will accelerate the decline and there is substantial scientific data to prove this, as we will see.

The Church of the Larger Solipsism and the Idolatry of Tolerance

U NITARIAN UNIVERSALISM TODAY is a liberal religion that characterizes itself by its focus on freedom of religion, tolerance, diversity and more recently multiculturalism, but in reality remains a largely aging, white, upper middle class group. The focus on reason in religion is virtually gone. Talk of truth or religious foundations are virtually gone and only the functional aspects of religion as therapeutic community are left. Most will tell you that community is the major and sometimes the only reason they belong. If religion is an attempt to answer the big questions in life; where did we come from, what is true, how do we live, what happens when we die, what is ethical, then Unitarian Universalism ironically has become a religion devoid of religion. It is all form and no content. The search for transcending thought has been minimized. The UUA remains devoted to social justice and some would say that the most universal characteristic is that almost all belong to the Democratic Party.

The drive towards immanence seems to be a buoy for people in the absence of evocative meanings within life itself. The new religious attitudes are dominated by a "reflexive spirituality" where "religious idioms become highly textured and multilayered; whatever else religion may be, in a mediated and consumption oriented society it becomes a cultural recourse broadly available to the masses. Responsibility falls more upon the individual -- like that of a bricoleur-- to cobble together a religious world from available images, symbols, moral codes, and doctrines" [45]

It is a religion that fits the narcissistic, commoditized tenor of the times in what might be termed "The church of the larger solipsism." Look at the "Build Your Own Theology" class which despite protestations implies the idea that metaphysical foundational beliefs are mere personal preferences. Ministers today in the UUA dare not challenge anyone's theological views, as it is viewed as being intolerant or not allowing people to grow by themselves. But as Diana Eck the founder of Harvard's Pluralism Project points out, "Tolerance can create a climate of restraint, but not a climate of understanding. Tolerance is far too fragile a foundation for a religiously complex society and in the world in which we live today, our ignorance of one another will be increasingly costly." [46]

The newest trend in the UUA is the call by many to move even more radically from mere tolerance to become the intentionally multiracial, multicultural religion. As the Rev. Dr. Paul Razor calls it in the spring 2010 *UU World*, it is to be "radically egalitarian... radically inclusive." [47] It calls for the goal to make the UUA uncritically embrace any and all religious traditions. In personal discussion with The Rev. Cheryl M. Walker, she uses metaphors to describe the changes in radical pluralism. "With a focus on tolerance we were trying to be the salad bowl, and now we need to move towards being the soup, not homogenized, but still tasting all the ingredients."

Personally, when I hear ministers proclaiming this gospel of pluralism, I still hear homogenization as the outcome and the blender whirring sort of drowns out any other message. I hear trying to be all things to all people and that there actually is a universal religion. There is no one size fits all religion and the dream of one is a dangerous utopian dream, no matter how seductive and moralistic the argument is made. We have been careless with language and careless with the truth.

All this is supposed to be acceptable by using the outside marketing consultants "standing on the side of love" mantra. A few years ago I knew the financial manager for the Jim Jones church who survived the mass suicide by being on a fundraising trip to the United States at the time. He told me, "You know, everything Jim said was about being in a community of love, and I never saw how much ugliness that talk of love covered." As a side note, Jim Jones was thankfully turned down as a UU minister by the Ministerial Fellowship Committee. Had he been fellowshipped it would have destroyed the UUA in short order.

Evolutionary psychology is a powerful tool to help understand the underlying forces within religion. It has found that we have powerful instincts to build binding moral communities that have helped tribes survive and thrive. In addition, priests and shamans have powerful drives for power and control and all of us are driven to believe the incredible. As the Latin saying goes, "Mundis vult decepi", or "The people want to be deceived." Outsiders I have interviewed cannot believe the lockstep, utopian thinking in the UUA today that very smart people inside it cannot see. The UUA high priests tell a wonderful moral story of radical tolerance, and we desperately want to believe this uplifting ethical vision, but it is as much out of touch with reality as faith healing.

Counterintuitive Studies Concerning Religion

F OR A SCIENTIFIC perspective, let's look at one of the most important sociological studies of religion by Finke and Stark in their book *The Making of Religion 1776 to 1994* which is subtitled, *Winners and Losers in our Religious Economy.* [48] With no state sponsorship of religion in America, the story is one of market competition between denominations for people's allegiance. What emerges from the data is a historic growth curve for each denomination that closely matches a classic business product life cycle. A slow growth inception is followed by a rapid increase, followed by a slow decline, followed by a long-term marginalization of market share. See the "Religious Denomination Life Cycle" below.

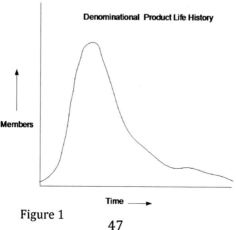

Denominational Product Life History

Members

Time ⟶

Figure 1

Denominational histories are remarkably similar in this history cycle. The data shows that growth is very fast at first when a sect is lay led, is perceived as a marginal sect or cult, is very narrow in its beliefs, promises high rewards for membership, demands a lot of time and financial commitment, and offers a comprehensive world view. This isn't the UUA. Denominations start their decline as they gain an educated professional ministry, which liberalizes the span of beliefs, as they and the congregations become more educated. The wider the theological view, the faster the decline will occur.

Denominations wither when there is little to distinguish one from another, and their coherent worldview starts to unravel. Members leave when membership does not seem to be very important to themselves or society. Why belong if it isn't important or unique? Their book ends with the line, "The primary feature of our religious history: the mainline bodies are always headed for the sidelines." This figure shows where denominations are today in their life cycle.

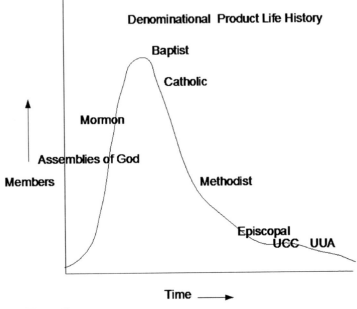

Figure 2

And that's where Unitarian Universalism is today, having seen its market share erode to virtual extinction. Despite the poetic, utopian vision of some that the UUA is the universalizing religion of the future, the reality is that it is an odd agglomeration of opposing visions without clear identity. The reality is that overt creeds or purposes do not shape a religion, but the subtle controls a leadership uses that make people feel either supported or neglected both personally and ideologically. Orthopraxy overwhelms orthodoxy.

There are always bell curve spectrums of adherents in a denomination on any perspective be it theism/humanism, rational/emotive, casual/formal, or credulous/skeptical. All religions have a bell curve spectrum of choices within them. Figure 3 shows how the gullibility of the general population has increased. Figure 4 shows how the theistic trend has changed over time broadening the population curve and moving to the theological right.

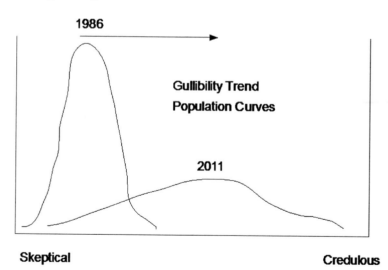

Figure 3

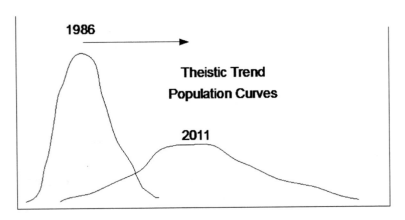

Non Theist   **Theist**

Figure 4

Population statistics tell us that all we can do is adjust two things - where the average members are within a larger spectrum of religions and how wide the bell curve of that spectrum. That's it. Rhetoric aside, a religion is defined by its ideological and functional midpoint and the breadth of views around that midpoint, most of which is controlled by subtle mechanisms such as language we talked of earlier.

Why Unitarian Universalism is Failing

U NITARIAN UNIVERSALISM IS theologically moving toward the overall mean of Christian denominations, while at the same time broadening its population spectrum. The theological midpoint is now closer to Theism/Christianity and the breadth continues to widen. This is a natural phenomenon as predicted by statistical science and the empirical data of Finke and Stark. But, according to their data, in this process of losing its uniqueness and a clear and powerful metaphysical claim, a religion dies. In the process known as regression to the mean, we see that natural forces push the UUA further to the conservative theistic viewpoint.

I was told by one UU minister that it was great that the Methodist religion and Unitarian Universalism were becoming so similar to each other as to be indistinguishable in the future. He regularly preaches at the old Christian congregation he came from. All mainline Protestant denominations have been losing members since the 1960s, between 25 and 40 percent according to the August 9, 2003 *Time* magazine article *Dead End for the Mainline*. Is this the UUA's model for success?

There is a dangerous underlying dogmatism that the UUA can be all things to all people and that trying to be more inclusive is a good marketing plan. The Stark and Finke study says this is a formula for brand elimination and denominational death. One only need look at the mainstream religions that we now want to emulate, Methodists, Episcopalians, Lutherans etc. which at one time waged wars over their differences. There isn't a dimes worth of difference between them now and today no one is going to die for any differences they may see. They have lost any vital center and create huge rationalistic tomes on better processes to gain members espousing group dynamics, better processing of new members, etc. They don't work. They don't work because they have nothing to sell and they continue to lose members to the non-denominational evangelical mega churches who do have something to sell. As the Rev.Khoren Arisian warns us, "Beware a ... movement ... that defines itself principally by promising a better process ... for then all real passion and substance will have been leeched from it."

Every study I have seen either denominationally or within an individual church reports the number one reason people belong to the UUA is to be with like-minded people. This is a totally normal human tribal response, but is in exact opposition to the UUA's stated goals which are focused on inclusiveness. In statistical terminology this equates with broadening the bell curve which history shows doesn't work. I have never seen a marketing plan where the primary need of the consumer was in opposition to the stated goals of the organization. It is a formula for failure.

If we were not hypocrites about promoting an indiscriminate pluralism we would open our doors and encourage fundamentalists of all stripes into our churches. If you have a visceral response to this proposal then I suggest all the talk of tolerance is just sweet sounding, manipulative rhetoric. Your ancient tribal voice is speaking to you. Some might say that most of them would not agree to the UU principles, but in fact many would agree to most of them.

The study by Starke and Finke shows that there is no substitute for answers to life's questions and for a bold, defined, alternative message. Maybe its Gresham's law applied to religion where bad ideas drive out the good ones or maybe just the general dumbed down society. Motiveless ambiguity will default us to the flattened bell curve of marginalized denominations. To look deeply means some might have to give up a giddy self referentiality for a view of religion that enjoins us to a more defined focus for religious truths.

If the UUA maintains its current direction I believe the data shows it will wither further into a faceless mediocrity. The UUA is becoming a one trick pony -- that of toleration. But, toleration is only one facet of a whole meaningful life and not one to which most of us are willing to devote ourselves exclusively. Pluralism does not answer the fundamental questions of religious existence, metaphysics and ethics, and is functionally conservative fearing real change and progress. Also, as the philosopher Robert Wolff pointed out, "Pluralism is fatally blind to the evils which affect the entire body politic, and as a theory of society it obstructs consideration of precisely the sorts of thoroughgoing social revisions which may be needed to remedy those evils." [48] Yes, even toleration can have a downside. And that is only part of our pluralism dilemma.

Pluralism

THERE IS ANOTHER conception of pluralism as espoused by the late philosopher Isaiah Berlin who coined the modern term. This pluralism holds the idea that "ultimate human values are objective, but irreducibly diverse, that they are conflicting and often uncombinable, and that sometimes when they come into conflict with one another they are incommensurable; that is, they are not comparable by any rational measure." Further, "The idea of a perfect society in which all genuine ideals and goods are achieved is not merely utopian; it is incoherent. All our great high liberal values including even the three pillars of liberalism, i.e. reason, freedom and tolerance are in radical irresolvable conflict." [49]

Religious life, like moral life, abounds in radical choice between rival goods and evils where reason leaves us in the lurch and whatever is done involves loss and sometimes tragedy. Berlin's is a tragic liberalism of unavoidable conflict, tradeoffs and irreparable loss among inherently competing values.

This is a Liberalism that while not succumbing to the total value relativism of Postmodernism, sees our differences as inherently irresolvable. Any universalistic claims are carryovers from logocentric, utopian, totalizing ideas be they Christianity, Marxism, Enlightenment Rationalism, turn of the 20th century modernist ideas, or the newer UU claims of a universalizing spiritual community. The limits of rational choice affirm the reality of radical choice.

Berlin's' conception of pluralism is, I believe, a deeper and ultimately more liberal one than the universalistic, egalitarian notion espoused by leadership of the UUA where tolerance is the highest value consuming and subsuming all other values including reason and critical thinking. Tolerance and diversity have become secular idols in the UUA. UU Christian minister Rev. Earl Holt called the phenomena, "Creeping creedalism."

The inherently competing nature of viewpoints means that radical, incommensurable minority viewpoints such as Humanism are always in danger of being displaced and co-opted by the majority theistic culture.

We cannot evade tradeoffs whatever is our focus. Focusing on the progressive, some would even say elitist dimensions, means necessarily ignoring some viewpoints. Conversely, the egalitarian focus ends up ignoring the more heretical, non-mainstream viewpoints (e.g. humanism and paganism). Harvard Divinity School, once the bastion of rational religion, tried this egalitarian social experiment, and is now dominated by theists of all varieties. While there may be short-term benefits, the dominant Judeo/Christian, faith based view will ultimately prevail as a tyranny of the majority takes place.

The irony is that by promoting indiscriminate pluralism, the UUA necessarily promotes the majority cultural position (theism) at the expense of the minorities who slowly learn to conform, assimilate, or leave. Minority positions only last if assiduously nurtured. Many think you can have it both ways, egalitarian and progressive religion, but this is a utopian hypothesis at odds with human nature. There is no "right" answer on what should be the focus of the UUA, as there are only hard choices and tradeoffs whose practical effects will determine whose religious views are nurtured and preserved.

The UUA advertises that it is the home for the free mind, but what is not said is that it is not the home for free speech. Everyone knows the unspoken rule today is of going along to get along, so self-censorship is the real rule; think about it, just don't say it unless it is some nice comforting platitude. There is an operating premise that we should not be openly critical of religion even when we know religion calls people to fly airliners into the World Trade Towers, genitally mutilate woman in Africa, hate homosexuals, seek psychic remedies to diseases, and deny global warming. Ideas have consequences, and we are complicit in these crimes when we do not see and take aim at faith-based religion itself, which is at the core of these ideas. In the words of Salman Rushdie, "What is freedom of expression? Without the freedom to offend, it ceases to exist."

There are some very practical, non-ideological reasons for the UUA to turn away from radial pluralism. David Niose points out in his book, *Nonbeliever Nation,* [50] that the rise of the religious right's political control in this country has continued unabated despite liberal dissent of specific agendas such as LGBT rights, abortion rights, woman's rights, economic justice, separation of church and state, and almost everything UU's hold dear. Liberalism has not only failed, but it has continually lost ground since the Moral Majority first burst onto the scene in the seventies. The failure has been due to the fact that no one has contested the religious right at its core – the whole validity of faith-based religion and expresses the idea as Christopher Hitchens said that religion poisons everything.

Showing intolerance to religion has been antithetical to Unitarian Universalism in recent years, but not in Humanism's glory days. Many in the antitheist movement claim liberal religion has been unwittingly supportive of the religious right as silence becomes a form of betrayal, tolerance becomes passive assent, and liberal religion is guilty of supporting irrational beliefs that inevitably leads to the religious right's excesses. Religious tolerance leads to accommodation with the worst actors in the religious landscape and they take advantage of liberals' good will. This is why the religious right has grown unabated as we never attack their faith. If ideas have consequences, recent history has given us empirical evidence of how religious tolerance can have unintended consequences.

The greatest UU scholar of the twentieth century, James Luther Adams, saw for himself the gutless, mute, liberal, tolerant, response to Fascism in Germany in the nineteen thirties. He saw Liberalism fail in its mission. It drove him to say, "An authentic prophet is one who prophesies in fashion that does not comfort people, but actually calls them to make some new sacrifices. That's an authentic prophet, whether one speaks in the name of God or whatever. A great deal of authentic prophetism in the modern world is to be found in non-religious terms and in non-church configurations, often even hostile to the church. The churches themselves have broadly failed in the prophetic function. Therefore a good deal of so-called atheism is itself, from my point of view, theologically significant. An authentic prophet can and should be a radical critic of spurious piety, of sham spirituality." [51]

Times have changed regarding criticism of religion. This is an age where one can see the popular response to a Broadway show like *The Book of Mormon* which can blast the Mormon faith as well as giving a positive Humanist message. In contrast, candid sarcastic religious criticism contained in a Broadway show would be viewed as intolerant and divisive in many UU churches today. If you can't see something is wrong here, that the UUA is no longer a truly free church when religious criticism is seen as intolerant, I don't know what more to offer. Only those too long immersed in the UU culture cannot see how a doctrinaire ideology now suppresses real thought and speech.

The "New Atheists" like Christopher Hitchens, Daniel Dennett, Sam Harris, and Richard Dawkins have challenged the traditional liberal religious tolerance model since it perpetuates the system of power, control and abuse that has done more harm than any other idea. As feminist activist Greta Christina points out, preventing critical talk of religion amounts to saying "shut up." She uses a speech titled, "Why Atheists Are Angry" to intentionally confront the "angry Atheist" put down with a list of 100 religious abuses. She points out that every social action movement needed those whose anger over abuses challenged and empowered the apathetic conservative nature we all share.

If the use of reason in religion in the UUA continues to diminish, it will further alienate the growing numbers of those who feel their religious integrity is compromised by the growing antiscientific domination of our neo-romantic culture. Humanist bashing, always prevalent in society at large, now is encouraged by many in what was one of the few homes for Humanists. Humanism is demonized, distorted and misrepresented as heartless rationalism, being overly critical, or "old school."

As the philosopher Noretta Koertge says, "Some rationalize that postmodern philosophy justifies their own lack of intellectual discipline and their prejudice to trash reason and humanism. It does not." [52]

As pointed out earlier, the UUA grew tremendously and was the fastest growing denomination with a bold focus on Humanism and the majority of lay members at least humanistic, if not Humanists. If filling UUA churches or becoming main stream is the goal, it can easily be done, as pointed out by the late Rev. Bob Kauffman, by merely changing the name to another denomination that avows individual freedom of belief, but with a different focus - the Baptists.

Even the names Unitarianism and Universalism were borne with a rejection of certain theological views. The historical mission has been to advance religious thought using the best of reason, compassion, and open-minded free thought. Those asking us to be the "Universal Religion" have noble social goals, but leave us with a utopian, superficial pluralism that does not honor the very real differences in our viewpoints and will not advance those social goals.

Can Unitarian Universalism Be Revived?

THE QUESTION OF whether the decline in the UUA can be stemmed is a troubling one and perhaps as a starting point it is helpful to look first at some of the strengths and weaknesses within the UUA so that one can build on the strengths and minimize the weaknesses. The great strength, the great identity of the UUA in the past was the focus on reason in progressive religion. Being part of the Boston Brahmin tradition of elitist religion had its benefits in that demographic sector. It limited the potential audience, but it had a premier cache and the benefit in many communities, as they say, of being the only show in town for those inclined toward strong rational liberalism. The UUA does not enjoy that distinction today and in fact went from carrying a label of "God's frozen people" to the religion of "'some nice people with a lot of flakes." Both labels carry the burden of an inaccurate stereotype, but do point toward certain proclivities of the times.

In the case of the generalization of being Rationalists at one time, at least there was no competition except for Ethical Culture and the Society of Humanistic Judaism. Today, as Rev. Sarah Oelberg said, "We are no longer God's frozen people as we were once accused; we have thawed out completely and are flowing willy nilly all over the place." [53] Today as the UUA presses toward the middle of the theological spectrum it encounters more competition from other hungry denominations including the Unity Church, Reformed Judaism, Buddhist temples, and liberal Christians such as the liberal wing of the Episcopal, Methodist, Lutheran and United Church of Christ. The field is crowded.

The greatest strength in the UUA ministry is the pastoral skills of its ministers. The ministry as a whole has well developed people skills critical to dealing with the politics of wide ranging theological viewpoints, and crucially in tending to the supportive life of others. While ministers a hundred years ago might spend forty hours a week researching and writing their sermons and possibly a few hours to parish duties, the modern minister has reversed the focus toward the interpersonal and organizational aspects of ministry. By and large the ministers in the UUA have exceptional interpersonal skills.

Another strength of the current ministry is a commitment to social justice and outreach. There is a high emphasis on LGBT rights which is not to be unexpected as 24% of the woman ministers describe themselves as lesbian or bisexual with immigration rights rising in importance. [54] There is no data on their male counterparts. Curiously there is no talk or action or social justice for non-believers. In fact at the 2011 General Assembly I asked the director of the "Standing on the Side of Love" campaign why they did not stand up for the discrimination against non-theists. He told me, "We don't see real discrimination there compared to the LGBT area." I was quite shocked as polls indicate Atheists as the most hated and discriminated minority in the US. The University of Minnesota study showed 49.6 % of people oppose Atheists while only 22.6 % oppose homosexuals. [55] Even Barney Frank can come out as a gay man, but not as the Humanist he is reported to be.

The commitment to liberal politics in general is such that some say the only real theology of the UUA is the Democratic party. Of course there are in fact Republicans, but they are extremely underrepresented. The demographics of political identification can be viewed as strength or weakness depending on which market the UUA seeks.

Other strengths in the UUA are the values regarding inclusiveness and toleration. A welcoming spirit really does infuse the congregations. Still, despite enormous efforts and focus to become multiracial, the UUA is still 89% white and actually decreased in black membership from 1.3% in 1997 to 1.0% in 2008. The focus on multiculturalism just isn't working. One answer for this may be as Meera Nanda in her book *Epistemic Charity of Social Constructivist Critics* [56] said, "What from the perspective of Western liberal givers looks like a tolerant, nonjudgmental, therapeutic 'permission to be different' appears to some of us 'others' as a condescending act of charity." The blacks that are attracted to Unitarian Universalism are the educated, suburban, high income professionals. This is not representative of the demographics within the African American community, forty percent of whom are evangelicals. In contrast it is interesting to note that the 2012 Reason Rally in Washington DC attracted around 25,000 mostly young and extremely diverse in race and gender, just the type of audience the UUA attempts to attract.

The skills within the UUA extend to excellent skills in community building. It should be noted that other denominations have well-developed skills in community building as well so the UUA is not unique in that regard and probably behind the mega churches.

The UUA market strength presently resides in the humanistically oriented, process theology, fuzzy theism, and new age demographic segment of the religious market. As mentioned earlier this is a sizable market today, but it is in competition with other religious venues and is unfocussed. In particular, the Unity Church has a central focus on the New Age market. More important, it is a market that is waning with aging baby boomers.

What are the weaknesses in the UUA today? Several have been mentioned earlier. The UUA has a tendency to latch onto a trend and hold onto it even when the culture has moved on. Today, holding onto the Postmodern viewpoint is not only outdated and intellectually shallow, but a drag on future growth. Another area where the UUA is holding onto a departing issue is the LGBT social action focus where the legal battle continues, but culturally the battle has been won with young adults and seems to be reaching a point of political resolution in the next couple of years. Most mainline denominations have welcoming congregations as well and in some ways are further along than the UUA. When forty-four percent of Evangelical youth today support LGBT marriage you know it is neither courageous nor a cutting edge social action issue as it once was. This is not to say there is not a lot of continuing work to do, but there will be diminished rewards as it is a social action issue that is on the backside of the curve of issues, and there are so many other pressing ones calling for the future. More important, anyone who has studied the LGBT issue knows it isn't a LGBT issue at its core, but a religious one. Religious indoctrination is what feeds the discrimination. And to repeat, discrimination of nontheists remains unchallenged despite the fact that if one denomination should be at the vanguard of non-theism support, it should be the UUA.

The biggest barrier to creating effective change is in the ministry. The drive away from Humanism and the use of critical intelligence came from the ministry and the leadership, not the laity. The UUA used to attract the best and the brightest into the ministry, but few would make that claim today. Today there are three demographic groups of ministers coming into fellowship. The first group, those right out of college, contain a good percentage of quality future potential ministers. The second are those moving from other denominations, and this can be a mixed bag. At one time this figure was pegged at 64%, but it may be much higher, but, to be fair, no reliable data could be found. Many are "castoffs," but are exactly the kind of awakened rebels that have always sustained the UUA. Many ministers from other denominations carry with them only what they know already and redirect themselves to a "Christianity light" message with some popular culture mixed in. They learn Unitarian Universalism on the fly and learn only a smattering of Humanism. One UCC minister told me that a joke in their denomination is that if it didn't work out there they could always become a UU.

The last group is more difficult to pin down accurately without appearing to build stereotypes. I say this as one who has studied the Meadville Lombard students and spoken to many ministers about this problem. It is the problem of the midlife career change to a calling in the ministry. In this group are many fine examples of those whose successful first careers gave them a skill set for success, but eventually had a calling for the ministry and its overarching high values. The ministry, though, is like many see in the psychological field where those trying to work through their own personal problems see the ministry as a way to heal and transform themselves. The wounded healing ministry model promotes this aspect of religion as therapy practice and in the process the congregations suffer. This is not a segment of our ministry that has a prophetic, rational voice nor can it elicit the best in critical reasoning. Some in this category are the emotionally crippled who have failed in other aspects of life and now weigh down a congregation rather than empower them. There are far too many of these toxic personalities and as a congregant I saw a number pass through our church in quick succession.

My point in the previous discussion is that today the ministry has few developed skills or even an interest in critical thinking, philosophy, science, or developing a foundational basis for religious beliefs. Returning to an association devoted to rational religion would be difficult at this point as the cultural capital and individual skills to accomplish this task have largely been lost. Making any changes of any sort would be difficult at this point. I asked Gene Kreeves, one of the pioneer Humanist ministers, what happened to the UUA ministry. He said, "They simply lost their nerve." Too many ministers today have lost or never had a prophetic voice and view the ministry as only a job to make people feel good in a healing community. Those that see a greater vision of progressive religion many times lack the courage of their convictions or the support of their fellow ministers. Fear keeps many "soft" humanist ministers from speaking out as there seems no upside in doing so.

The UUA has become a religion devoid of religion where the big questions, the staple of religion, are avoided at all costs. The result necessarily is a decline of ministerial religious and intellectual integrity. Under the cover of open-minded tolerance, any frank and explicit discussion about the big questions of life is sidestepped. Ministers and the membership are afraid to confront and affront anyone and appear dogmatic so they remain mute. Self-censorship about religion is more effective control than any cult could maintain. How many ministers would openly challenge the religious redefinition game? Not many.

There is a lack of courage or ability to defend a point of view, so emotionally manipulative, saccharine talk of love becomes the fall back position. Doctrinal positions become harder to defend in the new UUA so we are told that it doesn't matter what we believe, only how we act. But this begs the question. What is the basis for our ethics? What grounds our actions? As one learns in Rational Emotive Behavioral Therapy going back to the Stoics, we know don't just do things. Behind our actions we find that ideas create emotions which then create our behavior. Beliefs matter. Grounding matters.

For ministers, the advice is to keep it light to keep your job. Many ministers see the UUA in decline and see the issues, but they figure if they just keep it "religion light" that they can maybe make it to retirement. As before, follow the money to understand the situation.

In summary the UUA has strengths in its ability to build effective, intentional communities and has a ministry with good, but not unique, pastoral skills. Critical thinking skills largely have been lost. Most problematic is the lack of any focus or identity without which the UUA is lost.

The Transient and the Permanent in Unitarian Universalism

THE RECENT HISTORY shows that there isn't much in Unitarian Universalism that has proven permanent and this author will not argue for any. I will not argue that the present uncritical tolerance, fuzzy theism, humanistic model does not serve a significant segment of our population. I will not even argue that rational religion or Humanism must be revived in the UUA. What we can do is to consider the pragmatic consequences of alternative paths.

Each religion serves a particular market, but what the scientific data clearly shows is that the broader the market, the quicker the decline in membership. Whatever is done to stem the blood flow must involve moving from the ideology of indiscriminate pluralism to a more balanced set of values, but with a different intentional focus. This can be any focus, but without focus the UUA is lost. Having focus does not mean being dogmatic or building another ideology. It does not being intolerant. On many things we need to remain agnostic, but perpetual indecisiveness is not enlightenment, but neurosis. John Dewey called for knowledge grounded by warranted assertability. As Samuel Butler said, "Life is the art of drawing sufficient conclusions from insufficient premises."

The UUA has rightly already driven stakes in the ground regarding social and economic justice, religious liberty, LGBT rights, abortion, the Trinity, education, and a rejection of the bible as inerrant truths. Certainly there are some members who are not for abortion rights, economic justice, and LGBT rights, but no one can dismiss the reality of where the UUA stands on these issues. So the UUA is not as agnostic and inclusive as it might appear in principle. Let's assume that the focus became even more toward the experiential, "spiritual", therapeutic, emotional dimension of religion than it is now. There is benefit in this focus as it is already a major characteristic of the UUA today. It would just need to be more explicit and marketed accordingly.

One of the key marketing premises of membership organizations is that if you want to grow, look around and get more people that look like you. Focusing on the "fuzzy theism," experiential market at this point matches the current demographics. It would mean a slow continued withering of the Humanists on one end, and the definitive theists on the other, but an explicitly stated focus might revitalize the Association. The problem is that this demographic market segment appears to be on the wane.

It should be noted that the present explicit focus on making the UUA a multicultural organization is at direct odds with the rule of getting more people like you. No marketing plan could be more of a prescription for failure. The general Latino, Black and Asian population have little desire to be UU unless they are an upper middle class, politically liberal, suburban, and professional. A 1987 survey showed some interesting contrasts in the way African Americans value services. While 74% of UU's rated intellectual stimulation as the most important attribute in the UUA, the average African

American rated it at only 47% and are more inclined to pray and use the word God. Utopian thinking and political correctness means no one will call the leadership on this proposal. The curtain of the "holy of holies" of tolerance needs to be torn away so that tolerance can be placed on an equal altar with other high values.

Another focus could be a return to a focus on reason in religion as was the historical tradition. While this appeals to me as a Humanist, I see significant impediments because the capabilities for critical reasoning are diminished today within the ministry as well as the laity. In recent years, considerable time and talent have gone into internal discovery and little into reason and science about the world at large. These are disciplinary skills that are not easily attained or revived. Intellectual discipline is hard work compared to pop psychology and quoting the Dali Lama. Still, it could be possible if the leadership were enlightened, courageous, and motivated and an educational program were launched using books such as *How to Think About Weird Things* [57] and Carl Sagan's *Demon Haunted World* [58] in recommended classes. Better yet, some of the great online sources like the *Kids Without God* website and *Qualiasoup*. Some might ask what science has to do with religion. Richard Dawkins in *River out of Eden* [59] says, "Science shares with religion the claim that it answers deep questions about origins, the nature of life, and the cosmos. But there the resemblance ends. Scientific beliefs are supported by evidence, and they get results. Myths and faiths are not and do not."

Beyond the need for a better marketing program by possibly renewing a focus on reason in religion within the UUA, there is an overall ethical issue. The infatuation with Postmodernism's extreme cynicism and casting off of the focus on rational religion in the UUA was not just an unfortunate silly infatuation with trendy nonsense, but a deep Nihilistic rejection of all that makes humanity flourish. As Dietrich Bonhoffer wrote, "Contempt for the age of rationalism is a suspicious sign of failure to feel the need for truthfulness." [60]

Let's consider the option of a focus on Humanism. Before the Postmodern turn, as mentioned earlier, Meadville Lombard professor Robert Tapp and the 1965 Committee for Appraisal - *A Free Church in a Changing World*, saw the success of Humanism and more importantly science as an epistemological grounding for liberal religion and recommended that the UUA explicitly promote that focus. President Dana Greeley rejected the report and that recommendation was never implemented. Today the demographics in the general population of the UUA have turned.

The 2012 Pew study of religious affiliation [61] shows that the growth of the "nones" has been exponentially rising. Fully 19% now describe themselves as having no religious affiliation increasing from 15% in just five years and is greater than all the minority religions combined. Consider that ten years ago only 6% said so. One third of adults under thirty are religiously unaffiliated. Eighteen percent now doubt the existence of God. 49% say they seldom or never attend a religious institution. 15% say they are neither religious nor spiritual.

Studies in Europe show that once a generation is not brought up in the religious model, they rarely embrace it themselves. I believe the data shows the beginnings of this phenomenon in the US as well. If one skips a generation today without religion, it is doubtful if succeeding generations with return later. This is a good indication that the "I'm spiritual, not religious" group will diminish here as it has only been a safe way station to complete secularization in a religious dominant society. Once it is safe to be an atheist, one no longer needs any religious crutches.

While the UUA continues its decline, secular organizations such as the American Humanist Association, the American Atheist Association, the Freedom From Religion Foundation and other secular organizations have been growing three and four fold in the last few years.

The trend toward non-theism is expanding greatly, especially with the young. While an aging Unitarian Universalist Association holds onto New Age (now really old age) practices amongst baby boomers, I can attest that the new secular youth look at the UUA with amusement and are flocking to non-theist groups primarily through the Internet. The UUA is behind the curve as usual and missing a golden opportunity as Humanism's roots are in the UUA and future demographics are shifting dramatically in the secular direction. The sad irony is that while the UUA excels in building loving, nurturing communities with professional leadership, the Humanist chapters are in large part not skilled in building professional leadership or in building communities. The American Humanist Association Chapters and other secular groups I have been associated with are filling with young people and ex-UUA members who as they say didn't leave the UUA as much as it left them. Unitarianism filled the specific market for those wanting a community of reason in the past, but now that market is unfilled at a time when the immediate demand is there.

The United States appears to be heading toward the European cultural direction where virtually everyone describes himself or herself as a Humanist, but organizations for communities' sake have little pull for them. Most people still live within 50 miles of where they were born. Their community at large is their religious community where churches are little more than museums, and a confidential poll some years ago of Anglican ministers identified that 49% of them did not believe in God. The joke in Europe is that there are only three times people go to church any more and two of them they are carried in: hatching, matching and dispatching. Remarkably, even Ireland of all places is expected to see religion disappear, and only one priest was ordained last year. In Great Britain 850,000 weddings were performed last year by Humanist celebrants, more than all the other religions combined. The Norwegian Humanist Association has over 40,000 members. This is where the USA appears to be heading, and the UUA can take advantage of the secular tide in developed countries by moving toward an intentional secular focus.

Edwin Wilson, Unitarian Minister, coauthor of "Humanist Manifesto I," and founder of the AHA, told me one time that when he founded the AHA, he promised the Unitarian Association that he would not compete for members in building communities. He later regretted that decision when the UUA started rejecting Humanism and felt that the compromise he made as well as the earlier compromise the Western Conference made in staying in the Unitarian Association and not completing the schism were bad decisions in hindsight. Humanism in the UUA was eventually co-opted.

Humanism offers an evolving encompassing tradition based on both the best of the Enlightenment and Romantic movements providing a balance of the poetic/emotional, and the rational/empirical. It offers a web of belief that gives us real answers based on reality. As Carl Sagan said, "It is far better to grasp the Universe as it really is than to persist in delusion, however satisfying and reassuring."

Could the UUA return to a focus on Humanism as it did in its greatest growth period? It certainly could, but the hurdles of a leadership committed to the idolatry of tolerance and the convenient utopian fiction of egalitarianism are deeply imbedded. It is far too easy for leadership to just let things ride as they are than to rock the boat. Frankly, today there is no credible, open-minded intellectual position other than scientifically based naturalism, and time is on the side of Humanism. Supernaturalism is in its death throes in developed nations. Again, look at Europe. A recent study says that religion may become extinct in nine nations and is dropping dramatically in all major advanced nations. [62] Unitarianism may not survive unless it embraces again an explicit and unapologetic naturalism, gets ahead of this historical trend and stakes it as its territory.

New Age, Process Theological, vague spirituality, and "fuzzy theism" presently sells to many Baby Boomers, but holding onto that theological focus, staying on the backside of the curve, will mean the UUA will diminish along with that demographic population. Radical egalitarianism seems to be so dominant that no other focus is politically possible for the moment, but there is no vital center to it, and it has already proven to be a failing model. A golden opportunity exists right now for the UUA and the window is not yet closed. Can the UUA see this inevitable trend and capitalize on it?

Corporate marketer Aaron Burns says, "Marketing studies tell us there is a 'Tipping Point' in any brand's life cycle during the growth stage where sales accelerate (usually exponentially) due to a shift in a consumer's assessment of "perceived new trial risk. When the Tipping Point occurs, the brand is said to have established 'momentum.' What was formally (formerly?) 'New Trial Risk' (fear of the unknown) is almost instantly replaced by consumer intrigue and brand appeal, the next 'up and coming' thing. At this point, a consumer usually knows someone (within several degrees of separation) who has tried and embraced the brand, virtually eliminating 'New Trial Risk' through some kind of peer endorsement. Momentum is rising for the secular movement. At some point, everyone will know an active Humanist (within several degrees of separation), and that is usually when 'The Tipping Point' goes into full swing. With growing consumer intrigue, Humanism will become the next hot item." [63]

Look at John Stewart, Bill Mahr, South Park, Tim Minchin, and Penn Jillette as examples of popular media figures openly hostile to religion and you can see we are closing in on the tipping point. This will be further enhanced by the use of digital media as a source for information and peer endorsement.

If the UUA is to attract the booming secular youth, whole new models of community will need to be developed. The old religious model is dead. Secular youth find community and education in multivariate ways, tied into many virtual digital communities, not requiring a single intentional community, and certainly viewing ministers as offensive and an anarchic relic of religion's history of power and control. A "cafeteria style" community may be one community model of the future. Evangelical mega churches are already tying into these cultural revolutions experimenting with "twitter" churches, with online Facebook bulletins, small online groups, Youtube educational courses, blogs and small group meet-ups at local venues. It is still too early to tell what models will work in the future, but these experimental attempts seem to be on the right track.

One can look back nostalgically at the old models, but that will only delay the time of reckoning. As they say, the trend is your friend, and at this critical juncture we cannot afford to look back as the religio-secular revolution that is occurring will build momentum as all cultural revolutions do. We don't want to be left in histories wake. Evangelicals with their tremendous ability to detect and adjust to trends could win the battle of the new marketing paradigm, or possibly we could end up with a totally secular culture as in most of Europe led by countries like Denmark, Norway and Sweden. In this scenario our churches become fashionable restaurants, discos and museums. Mathematical models show religion being driven to extinction [64] especially as the world becomes wealthier as there is a linear relation between poverty and religion with the USA being the sole outlier. [65] Time is short.

The education and background of the ministry would be difficult to change unless dynamic, courageous leadership developed that was brave enough to confront the status quo and envision a secular future for the UUA. Any changes will only come from courageous parish ministers willing to stand up for a prophetic message in opposition to the entrenched bureaucratic leadership firmly wed to the present ideology. Parish ministers will determine the future viability of the UUA. It happened before with the ministers of the Western Conference who saw the future, acknowledged a scientific world view, and challenged everyone in spite of an entrenched hierarchy. It can only happen with the youth today unless we give up the religious language redefinition game. It just will not work with much of the millennial generation.

We can revive the UUA. It can happen again. Real change will only come from the power in the pulpit and the power of polity. Individual courageous, visionary, ministers will have to take bold steps to announce and promote focused agenda churches and ignore the Boston dogma under the rule of polity. When the first congregation announces under the rule of polity that they are intentionally focusing on reason in religion and Humanism again, while honoring freedom of conscience, building new models of community, others will follow.

It is crucial to understand that most of what we would be talking about going forward is primarily a difference in degree, not substance for the UUA at large. The criticism will be that what I am arguing for is theological dogmatism and closing of the free mind. It can be an effective "straw man" that I do not relish having to knock down. No one will tell people they can't come across with certain views. No one would exclude anyone. In reality we all self-exclude and vote with our feet if our needs are not met. As population statistics and the earlier study by Stark and Finke shows, we tend to stay in populations like ourselves. We are all tribal social bigots to some extent seeking to be around others like ourselves and conversely wanting some diversity. That is why the only things we can really control are the midpoint of the population and the breadth around it. We all have our comfort level on both how different the group is from us and how much diversity we can handle. It is only human nature. To make religion a binding force it needs some coherence.

The way to change the midpoint is not through overt ways, but more subtly as it has always been done. If you teach classes on new age spirituality in the church, guess what audience you attract? If you teach classes on critical thinking or the basis of emotions in ethical decisions from Evolutionary Psychology guess what group you attract? If your sermon includes some of the great cosmological insights from Laurence Krauss's new book *A Universe out of Nothing* [66] you will attract one audience, and if you quote the total manipulative nonsense of Deepack Chopra you will get another.

If you preface the word Humanism with the adjective "fundamentalist" as the minister does in one church, people get the "dog whistle" message. If you talk of our rich history of reason in religion you again shift the demographics over time.

Again, we can only control two things, the theological midpoint and the breadth of the congregants around that midpoint. That's it. All we can do is shift the population curve right or left and make it narrower or wider regardless of what direction we want to go. It is an understanding of simple population statistics shorn of the flowery rhetoric we all tend to use and that is how we have always evolved our message. It is how the UUA can recreate and transform itself today by becoming more focused and taking advantage of the secular move in our culture by moving the population to the secular pole. It can save the UUA for the future and take advantage of the secular trend.

Visioning What Could Be

THERE IS A "wholeness hunger" out there with the belief that secular and religious narratives have failed. Excursions into hedonism, crass consumerism, drugs, therapeutic self-help groups, new age, spirituality, and career advancement haven't erased the hollowness for many. Modern culture seems to be a failed habitat for meaning in the absence of an evocative whole story.

We cannot slip into some utopian simplicity when faced with the dilemmas of our conflicting high values. Almost always there are loses. When some Unitarian Universalists believe that there is no downside to total pluralism, or conversely some rationalists insist on contesting every irrational belief, I cringe. Yet, those sorts of absolutism are maintained with the pretense that there are not real dilemmas in which we must choose or let the natural forces of disintegration take place. Motiveless ambiguity will default the UUA to the flattened bell curve of marginalized denominations. To look deeply means some might have to give up a giddy self-referentiality for a functional view of religion that enjoins us to a community search for secular truths that openly acknowledges again that supernatural foundations have been discredited and deal with the world as it is in the context of naturalism.

As the Rev. Stefan Jonasson says, "Our New England fore-bears imagined their faith as creating a shining 'city on the hill.' Sadly, we have allowed the core of that city to atrophy while fleeing to its idiosyncratic suburbs. In some ways, Unitarian Universalism has come to resemble sprawling sub-urbs, without a healthy urban core." [67] The leadership of the UUA who have led us to this point are all good, decent, smart people, but falling into a narrow, unsupportable ideology they have led the UUA to a utopian world with a darkening future.

We are entering a collision of the unsustainable and the untenable. If some think a radical change in the present direction is untenable, then I ask for an explanation of what data there is to justify the unsustainable decline by staying with the present focus on radical egalitarianism. The data shows clearly that the best chance for reviving the UUA is in fulfilling our original mission focusing on reason in religion and meeting the burgeoning demands of a secular society.

I do not believe the UUA will be judged by how many members it has, although there is a real danger of the Uni-tarian Universalist Association dissolving in our lifetimes. Paraphrasing Carl Sagan, history will judge the UUA in three ways; the courage of our questions, the depths of our answers and how we actually live our lives. What none of us wants to admit is that real growth and change involves discipline, confrontation and yes, pain. The recent Unitarian Universal-ist conservative, non-confrontational direction lacking any prophetic vision must be challenged or the UUA is lost. We can mask these issues with self-righteous piety, but with no compelling prophetic vision, no Promethean urge, no vital center it will wither. Without courage and integrity what purpose is there for the UUA?

The Unitarian and the Universalist churches were built on rejection of worn out, unsubstantiated ideas of the Trinity and eternal damnation. At some point you have to say the jury now finds certain truths as untenable. Truth is what's left after we get rid of all the lies. How is it the UUA cannot at this point have the intellectual courage to say that from all we know Evolution is undeniable and part of our doctrine and seriously promote it? As early as 1860 Rev. Newton Mann, a minister in Cincinnati, gave a sermon on the thoroughgoing implications of Darwin's *Origin of Species* "predicting a revolutionary effect on all provinces of thought particularly Biblical theology and the psychology of religion and ethics." [68] The importance of Darwinian thought cannot be overemphasized as philosopher Daniel Dennett says that evolution has become a "universal oil" dissolving all philosophical questions. No part of our lives is not in some way illuminated by evolutionary insights.

A hundred years ago the patriarch of modern Humanism, John Dietrich, professed an unapologetic Humanism and in his pulpit could give a sermon called, *The Folly of Half-Way Liberalism* in which he said that he was "ashamed ... of the complacency ... from a reactionary leadership of those who assume to wear the mantle of religious liberalism, yet who - either through a caution borne of worldly ambitions, or through a mind enfeebled by the lack of intellectual discipline, or through a soul too weak to bear the rigors of an open sea – persist in giving comfort to all those forces of reaction that have bound their souls in the horrible shackles of fear and darkness." [69] He faced the same issues we do today, but had the courage to stand up for the force of progressive Humanist thought.[70]

The lowest common denominator is not what the membership seeks, but rather communities that prophetically challenge and nurture our growth without compromising our religious and intellectual integrity. Sometimes that may mean intentional communities where minority religious views are unapologetically promoted and protected from the onslaught of popular religion and culture.

A religion based on radical egalitarianism and radical inclusiveness trying to placate everyone has resulted in the abandonment of the responsible search for truth and meaning in favor of self-censorship. A religion offering only intentional communities is a poor substitute for answering the fundamental questions of existence. Feel good religion is like a quick hit of cocaine producing an ecstatic buzz and then a quick let-down. The short-term rewards are great, but it still leaves one hungry for something more substantial in the long term. We have become superficial dilettantes nervously moving between many traditions, all the while our hearts long for an integrated whole view of life that matches with reality.

We long for a vital center to our lives that both grounds us and inspires us, a vision of grander authenticity to our lives and not just smaller truths. All of us long for an evocative whole story and higher vision that lifts our hearts, pushes us to higher meanings, and ennobles our lives. Some may find that integrated story for the future of the UUA is already there in the balanced secular life of here and now, of heart and mind, reason and compassion, accepting the exhilarating challenge of moving again toward a responsible search for truth and meaning.

Notes:

1. John Kekes, *Against Liberalism*, Ithaca, NY: Cornell University Press, 1997, p. 4

2. Charles H. Lyttle, *Freedom Moves West: A History of the Western Unitarian Conference 1852-1952*, Boston: Beacon Press, 1952, p. 186

3. Earl Morse Wilbur, *Our Unitarian Heritage 3rd ed.*, Boston: Beacon Press, 1925, p. 468

4. Unitarian Universalist Association, *The Free Church in a Changing World; The Reports of the Commissions for the Churches and Fellowships of the Unitarian Universalist Association*, 1963 p. 28

5. David Robinson, *The Unitarians and the Universalists*, Westport CT: Greenwood Press, 1985, p. 177

6. Lyttle, *op. cit.*, p. 190

7. *Preliminary Reports of the Commission of the Free Church in a Changing World*, Unitarian Universalist Association, 1961, p. 31

8. The Quality of Religious Life in Unitarian Universalist Congregations - A *Survey by the Commission on Appraisal, 1989,* pp. 6-7

9. *The Commission on Appraisal, Membership Statistics Interim Report*, Unitarian Universalist Association, 1992, p. 10

10. The Commission on Appraisal, *Interdependence*, Unitarian Universalist Association, 1997, estimated during commission hearings.

11. Robinson, *op. cit.*, p. 171

12. *Ibid.*, p. 178

13. *Report of the Committee on Goals*, Unitarian Universalist Association, 1967, p. 25

14. Center for Free Inquiry, *Free Inquiry Magazine,* Buffalo, NY., March 2000

15. Carl Sagan, *Demon Haunted World*, New York: Ballantine Books, 1995, p. 6

16. Richard Hofstadter, *Anti-Intellectualism in American Life*, New York: Vintage Books, 1963, p. 24

17. Richard Evans, *Postmodernism and History*, Butterflies and Wheels, 2003

18. Alan Sokal and Jean Bricmont, *Fashionable Nonsense: Postmodern Intellectuals' Abuse of Science*, New York: Picador Press, 2001

19. Terry Eagelton, *Literary Theory: An Introduction*. Minneapolis: University of Minnesota Press, 1983

20. Terry Eagelton, *After Theory*, New York: Perseus Books, 2003

21. The Commission on Appraisal, *Engaging Our Theological Diversity*, Boston: Unitarian Universalist Association, 2005, p. 68

22. Ann Garry and Marilyn Pearsall, *Woman, Knowledge and Reality*, Boston: Unwin Hyman, 1989

23. Susan Jacoby, *The Age of American Unreason*, New York: Vintage Books, 2009

24. Unitarian Universalist Association, *Leaping from our Spheres - The Impact of Woman in the Ministry*, 2007

26. Paul Tillich, *The Courage to Be*, New Haven: Yale University Press, ISBN 0-300-08471-4 (2nd ed), 1952

27. Howard Radest, *Toward a Common Ground*, New York: Fredrich Unger, 1969

28. John Dewey, *A Common Faith*, New Haven: Yale University Press, 1934

29. Gabriel Vahanian, *The Death of God*, New York: George Braziller, 1961

30. Rem B.Edwards, *Reason and Religion*, Lanham, MD: University Press of America, 1979

31. John Cobb and David Griffin, *Process Theology: An Introductory Exposition*, Philadelphia: Westminster Press, 1976

32. Barry Kosmin and Seymour Lachman, *One Nation Under God*, New York: Harmony Books, 1993

33. Harold Bloom, *The American Religion*, New York: Simon and Schuster, 1992

34. R. Laurence Moore, *Selling God*, Oxford: Oxford University Press, 1994

35. Wade Clark Roof, *Spiritual Marketplace*, Princeton NJ: Princeton University Press, 1999, p. 4

36. Robert Bellah, *Habits of the Heart*, New York: Perennial Library, 1985

37. Henry Hitchens, *The Language Wars: A History of Proper English*, New York: Farrar, Strauss and Giroux, 2011

38. Joseph Epstein, Book Review of *The Language Wars: A History of Proper English*, Claremont Review of Books, 2011

39. John A. Buehrens and F. Forrester Church, *Our Chosen Faith*, (first ed.) Boston: Beacon Press, 1989, p.159

40. Adorno, T. W., with Max Horkheimer, *Dialectic of Enlightenment*. Trans. Edmund Jephcott. Stanford: Stanford University Press, 1944

41. John A. Buehrens and Rebecca Ann Parker, *Liberal Religion is Not Just a Compromise*, Boston: Beacon Press, 2010

42. Robert Latham, *Does Unitarian Universalism Have a Future?* Unpublished sermon

43. David Bumbaugh, "The Marketing of Liberal Religion," *Journal of Liberal Religion*, Chicago Vol. 9, January 8, 2009, http://www.meadville.edu/uploads/files/144.pdf

44. J. O. Prochaska, J. C. Norcross, C.C. DiClemente, *Changing for good: the revolutionary program that explains the six stages of change and teaches you how to free yourself from bad habits*. New York: W. Morrow, 1994

45. Roof, op.cit., p. 75

46. Diana Eck, *A New Religious America,* San Francisco: Harper Collins, 2001 p. 34

47. *Theological Implications*, Unitarian Universalist Association, *UU World*, Paul Razor (Spring 2010), p. 18

48. Roger Finke and Rodney Stark, *The Churching of America, 1776-1990,* New Brunswick, NJ: Rutgers University Press, 1992

49. Robert Paul Wolff, Barrington Moore Jr., Herbert Marcuse, *A Critique of Pure Tolerance* Boston: Beacon Press, Boston MA, 1967

49. John Gray, *Isaiah Berlin*, Princeton: Princeton University Press,1996, "Introduction"

50. David Niose, *Nonbeliever Nation*, New York: Palgrave Macmillan, 2012

51. James Luther Adams, in George K. Beach (ed.) *The Prophethood of All Believers,* Boston: Beacon Press, 1986, p. 57

52. Noretta Koertge, *A House Built on Sand*, New York: Oxford Press, 1998

53. Sarah Oelberg, *Spirituality Without God*, Unpublished sermon, Feb. 9, 2003

54. Unitarian Universalist Association, *Leaping from our Spheres- The Impact of Woman in the Ministry*, 2007

55. Gervais, W.M., Shariff, A.F., Norenzayan, A. *Do you believe in atheists? Distrust is central to anti-atheist prejudice.* J Pers Soc Psychol. 2011 Dec 101(6): pp.1189-1206.

56. Meera Nanda, *The Epistemic Charity of the Social Constructivist Critics of Science and Why the Third World Should Refuse the Offer,* New York: Oxford Press, 1998

57. Theodore Schick Jr. and Lewis Vaughn, *How to Think About Weird Things*, New York: McGraw Hill, 2003

58. Carl Sagan, *The Demon Haunted World--Science as a Candle in the Dark*, New York: Random House, 1995

59. Richard Dawkins, *River Out of Eden*, New York: Basic Books, 1995, p. 33

60. Dietrich Bonhoeffer, *Ethics*, SCM Press, Touchstone edition, 1995

61. Pew Forum on Religion & Public Life, *Religious Affiliation*, Washington, DC, 2012

62. Jason Palmer, "Religion May Become Extinct in Nine Nations," BBC news, March 22, 2011.

63. Aaron Burns, Personal communication, 2012

64. Daniel M. Abrams and Haley A. Yaple, "A Mathematical Model of Social Group Competition with Application to the Growth of Religious Affiliation", *Physics and Society*, January, 2011.

65. Gallup Research, *Religiosity is Highest in World's Poorest Nations*, 2010

66. Lawrence Krauss, *A Universe from Nothing: Why There Is Something Rather than Nothing*, New York: Free Press, 2012

67. Stefan Jonasson, Unpublished Sermon, *Let us Reason Together*

68. Lyttle, *op. cit.*, p. 265

69. John Dietrich, *What if the World Went Humanist - Ten Sermons*, Yellow Springs, OH: Fellowship of Religious Humanists, 1989, p. 46

70. Robert Tapp, *Religion among the Unitarian Universalists: Converts in the Stepfathers' House*, New York: Seminar Press, 1973

About the Author

MICHAEL WERNER IS an ardent Humanist and Unitarian Universalist having been past President of the American Humanist Association, Vice President of the Fellowship of Religious Humanists, President of the Humanist Foundation Fund, President of the Unitarian Church of Charlotte, a founder of SMART recovery, and an adjunct faculty member of the Humanist Institute. He supports a balanced Humanism of heart and mind, reason and compassion and a Unitarian Universalism that helps us discover how to be more fully human.

Starting Point Questions for Discussion Groups

1. What are your views about dilemmas and how do you handle tradeoffs between several high values?

2. What focus if any should the UUA have?

3. How do you emotionally handle debate and dissent?

4. Where, in a spectrum of one to ten, do you identify yourself regarding:

    Reason
    Experientialism
    Supernatural God belief
    Science as a way of knowing
    Importance/ability to discover of truth
    Elitism vs. Egalitarianism
    Toleration
    Religious Language Redefinition
    Religion as personal vs. a community search

5. Are the big religious questions important anymore?

6. How can the UUA grow and prosper?

7. Can there be a universal religion?

8. What are the Prophetic challenges today and tomorrow for the UUA?

9. What is more important, supportive intelligence or critical intelligence?

10. Should the UUA move toward a return to a focus on reason in religion?

11. How should the UUA respond to the secular revolution?

12. Does the UUA have a covenant? If so what and to whom?

CPSIA information can be obtained at www.ICGtesting.com
Printed in the USA
BVOW030947180613

323621BV00001B/2/P